Jewish Portraits, Indian Frames

BRANDEIS SERIES ON JEWISH WOMEN

Shulamit Reinharz, *General Editor*
Joyce Antler, *Associate Editor*
Sylvia Barack Fishman, *Associate Editor*
Susan Kahn, *Associate Editor*

The Brandeis Series on Jewish Women is an innovative book series created by the Hadassah International Research Institute on Jewish Women at Brandeis University. BSJW publishes a wide range of books by and about Jewish women in diverse contexts and time periods, of interest to scholars, and for the educated public. The series fills a major gap in Jewish learning by focusing on the lives of Jewish women and Jewish gender studies.

Marjorie Agosín, *Uncertain Travelers: Conversations with Jewish Women Immigrants to America*, 1999

Rahel R. Wasserfall, *Women and Water: Menstruation in Jewish Life and Law*, 1999

Susan Starr Sered, *What Makes Women Sick: Militarism, Maternity, and Modesty in Israeli Society*, 2000

Pamela S. Nadell and Jonathan D. Sarna, editors, *Women and American Judaism: Historical Perspectives*, 2001

Ludmila Shtern, *Leaving Leningrad: The True Adventures of a Soviet Émigré*, 2001

Jael Silliman, *Jewish Portraits, Indian Frames: Women's Narratives from a Diaspora of Hope*, 2001

Judith R. Baskin, *Midrashic Women*, 2002

ChaeRan Y. Freeze, *Jewish Marriage and Divorce in Imperial Russia*, 2002

Mark A. Raider and Miriam B. Raider-Roth, *The Plough Woman: Records of the Pioneer Women of Palestine*, 2002

Elizabeth Wyner Mark, editor, *The Covenant of Circumcision: New Perspectives on an Ancient Jewish Rite*, 2003

Kalpana Misra and Melanie S. Rich, *Jewish Feminism in Israel: Some Contemporary Perspectives*, 2003

Farideh Goldin, *Wedding Song: Memoirs of an Iranian Jewish Woman*, 2003

Jewish Portraits, Indian Frames

Women's Narratives from a Diaspora of Hope

Jael Silliman

BRANDEIS UNIVERSITY PRESS
Published by University Press of New England
Hanover and London

BRANDEIS UNIVERSITY PRESS
Published by University Press of New England,
37 Lafayette Street, Lebanon, NH 03766

Printed in the United States of America   5 4 3 2 1

First Brandeis/University Press of New England paperback edition 2003.
Originally published in cloth in 2001 by Brandeis/University Press of New
England in arrangement with Seagull Books, Calcutta, India.

Library of Congress Card Number 2001093447
ISBN 1–58465–305–1

Cover portrait of Flower Silliman by Harvey Chew
Photograph courtesy the author

For sale within the United States of America and Canada only

Photograph credits:

p. 1 courtesy Anita (Mordecai) Blackman

pp. 11, 14, 31, 107 (below), 125 (top left) by David Mordecai. Used by permission of Esthere Maelzer, Anita (Mordecai) Blackman and Cheryl (Mordecai) Isaac. © Estate of David Mordecai. For further information on David Mordecai's photographs, contact Anita (Mordecai) Blackman at <AnitaLee10@aol.com> or Cheryl (Mordecai) Isaac at <cheryl@custom-cakes.co.uk>

pp. 25, 57, 99, 121, 122, 125 (above right), 131, 132 courtesy Flower Silliman

p. 42 (above right) courtesy Tilly and Alston Zachariah; (below) courtesy Emma Rubin

p. 64 courtesy Michal Minster

p. 69 (below) by Randall Adair, courtesy Raz Joshua

p. 107 (above) courtesy Charles Joshua

p. 125 (below) courtesy Rabbi Ezekiel Musleah

P. 131 by Randall Adair

p. 159 by Amitava Bhattacharjee, courtesy the author

p. 165 courtesy Charles Solomon

pp. 173, 174 by Rono Palchowdhury, courtesy the author

For my mother, Flower, without whom this book could not have been written. To Amitava, Shikha and Maya for their inspiration, love and support in everything I do.

Contents

Acknowledgements

I am deeply indebted to my mother, Flower Silliman, without whose knowledge of the community and willingness to share it with me, this book could not have been written. Rabbi Ezekiel Musleah, an authority on the Jews of Calcutta and an old family friend, shared a great deal of information with me and was always encouraging and thoughtful in his response to my many queries and requests. Other members of the extended family and friends looked at several drafts of the book and provided me with insights, further information and corrections.

I have worked closely with wonderful editors. Christi Merrill set me on the right path in the early stages of my writing. Carolyn Brown suggested major rearrangements and the book took its final form in her capable hands. Christi and Carolyn enabled me to write from the heart and develop a voice of my own. Phyllis Deutsch from the University Press of New England gave me important pointers on the style I should strive for, and Lynn Lu, formerly of Southend Press, commented on an early draft. Anjum Katyal of Seagull Books, Calcutta, with her careful eye and attention to detail gave the finishing touches to the book. I want to say a special 'thank you' to each one for their contributions which were critical in the various phases through which this book has moved.

The University of Iowa and Iowa City have been very nurturing places. My ideas have developed substantially through the support of and interactions with numerous colleagues and students. I am particularly indebted to Anne Donadey and Laura Donaldson for their close reading, critical comments and references. They have been invaluable colleagues and friends throughout this process. Natasa Durovicova, Paul Greenough, Philip

Lutgendorf, and Anne Hardgrove (now at University of Texas, San Antonio) saw this project in many phases. They gave me suggestions at crucial points and provided a great deal of intellectual and moral support. Susan Schechter, Rosemary Scullion, Margery Wolf, Ellen Lewin and colleagues like Shelley Feldman, Kathy Hansen, Jon Stratton and Saurabh Dube, Shashi Tharoor, Shira Saperstein, Pratyusha Basu and Allen Roberts commented on selected chapters. Fiona Young and Vidya Kalaramadam, both graduate students in Women's Studies, worked closely with me, providing on-going technical and research assistance without which I could not have completed this project. Laura Kastens, also from Women's Studies, and Mindy Tuttle from Information Technology Services, helped way beyond the call of duty in extricating me from what seemed like never-ending computer glitches and conundrums.

There were many other ways in which this community supported this endeavour. I received invaluable funding from the Arts and Humanities Initiative and the Old Gold Fellowship—both awards from the University of Iowa. I was invited to present portions of this work in classes, workshops and seminars on campus. Paul Ingram of Prairie Lights Bookstore, Janice Baumback, Anne White and others in the wider Iowa City community, who know about books and writing, offered me all kinds of tips and advice.

I am blessed with having a wonderful family and friends who give of themselves and their time. My husband Amitava has always urged me forward and been there for me at anxious moments. His high standards and dedication to his work have been a source of inspiration throughout my career. My daughter Shikha often served as an in-house editor and critical commentator. I admire her passion for learning, enquiring mind and her skilful writing. My younger daughter, Maya, was indulgent with her time and trusted that I was doing something worthwhile. My sister Michal Minster paid special attention to the religious details I mention, with which I am less familiar. My cousin Raz Joshua also provided early encouragement and many anecdotes. My sister-in-law Anannya Bhattacharjee, and my brother-in-law S. Shankar made many useful suggestions at crucial junctures and helped in trimming the manuscript. They have been family, friends, critics and sparring intellectual partners all rolled into one.

My closest friends in Calcutta, Susmita Ghosh, Anita Mansata, Kalpana Palchowdhury and Anuradha Chatterji, critiqued my sketch and read several versions of this book. Rono Palchowdhury came with me to the synagogues at short notice to take the photographs I wanted. I thank each of them for their support and for making Calcutta home and such a special place for me.

A special thank you to Cheryl (Mordecai) Isaac, Anita (Mordecai) Blackman, Charlie Solomon, Moses Moses, Emma Rubin, Tillie Zachariah and Ethel Shayne of the Calcutta Jewish community and Gary Tartakov of Iowa State University for the photographs they so generously allowed me to use. I thank Naveen Kishore of Seagull Books for the layout and design of the book. The photographs and design have added a great deal of charm to the volume.

I am delighted to have this book published simultaneously in the United States and Calcutta. From the outset, it was very important to me that it be easily available in India; and through the University Press of New England, I hope to reach American audiences interested in Jewish Studies, Women's Studies, South Asian Studies, and other academic colleagues.

This is a long list of sincere thanks to family, friends, and colleagues whose contributions have made a significant difference to this book and meant a great deal to me.

Preface
Narratives of Diaspora

$\mathcal{A}$ MONTH BEFORE PESACH (PASSOVER), under the scorching Calcutta sun, there is a great deal of hustle and bustle in the compound of the Beth-el synagogue. Temporary bamboo and leaf structures shield matzah-makers busy at work. Poorer Jewish women sit on low wooden stools adeptly kneading, pummelling, and moulding unleavened dough. The wheat for the dough has been specially grown up-country, following halachic laws, and is brought to Calcutta for this annual ritual. Another group of women sit cross-legged on the ground rolling out the dough balls. Their wooden rolling pins and the large marble slabs on which they work are used only during Passover. The flattened dough rounds, fifteen inches in diameter, are collected quickly to be baked before the dough can rise.

Jewish men place coals in the fire to light the tandoors (clay ovens) built each year on the synagogue premises. Learned men from the community supervise the entire production to make sure that the rules of the Matzah Board are strictly observed. Jewish families, buying and weighing matzahs, fill the courtyard. They exchange news, gossip, and discuss their Pesach preparations. The Matzah Board makes free matzahs available to the poorer members of the community so that no Jew will go without during the festival. Thin and brittle matzahs lie one atop the other to be weighed on huge wooden and rope scales. After being weighed, stacks of matzahs are placed in shallow cane baskets. Some of the precious cargo is sent to Jewish homes by horsecart and rickshaw. Coolies, too, hoist the baskets atop their heads and make their way with their light but unwieldy loads through busy Calcutta streets to deliver the goods intact.

There was a thriving Jewish community in Calcutta in the nineteenth and first half of the twentieth century. At the beginning of the twenty-first century, only a handful of elderly Baghdadi Jews remains. A few matzahs are still made locally by non-Jews (supervised by Jews) for the Jews who are left. Very soon matzahs will no longer be made in Calcutta. The Jewish community will exist only as a memory, though a few impressive structures mark the Jewish presence. Many of the community institutions and the stately synagogues they built continue to run on Jewish trust funds. The Jewish Girls' School, once the centre of community life, has no Jewish girls attending it. It has been increasingly difficult for the synagogues to attain a minyan—the ten men required to conduct a service. The imposing edifices and physical spaces that denote a Jewish presence are hollow, for they are bereft of the people and social relations that gave them their purpose and meaning.

How did the Baghdadi Jews come to settle in Calcutta and why did they leave this city where they lived and prospered for more than a hundred and fifty years? Why did they leave a place where they knew no anti-Semitism and where they played an important role in the city's economic development? Baghdadi Jews lived and traded in small Jewish communities across the Middle East for many centuries. In the eighteenth century British imperial policies opened up economic opportunities in India and the Far East and Jews of the Middle East took advantage of them. By the nineteenth century they forged Jewish communities in the area stretching from Basra to Shanghai. Rather than generalizing about Baghdadi Jewish culture or cultural institutions I trace the development of this diaspora through the prism of four generations of women in my family.[1] The family portraits convey a sense of what it meant to be a woman of the diaspora in what I call 'Jewish Asia', within the frame of successive historic moments. The sketches of these women's everyday lives—from the social and political relationships they forged to the food they ate and the clothes they wore—trace the evolution of a community and underline the syncretic and dynamic nature of culture. For as feminist writer Meredith Tax reminds us, culture is 'the food we put on the table; the way we cook it; . . . the relationship between the people who sit at the table and the people who cook and serve; . . . what is discussed during the meal; what music, dancing, poetry or theatre accompany it; the social and the spiritual values of those present—for when we say culture, we include the visions, dreams and aspirations of humanity.'[2]

The first portrait is of Farha, my maternal great-grandmother. Her life epitomizes what it meant to live as part of a diaspora in the traditional sense of the term. Farha dwelled almost exclusively in the Baghdadi Jewish community no matter whether she was in Calcutta, Rangoon, or Singapore. The next portrait is of my maternal grandmother, Miriam (who called herself Mary). Mary also dwelled predominantly in this Baghdadi Jewish world, though she was a great deal more Anglicized than Farha and deeply influenced by British colonial practices. Whether in Sydney, London, or Jerusalem, Mary was part of the tight-knit Calcutta Jewish community. Her portrait highlights the roles that women played in relocating community as the diaspora shifted from its base in Calcutta to new sites. During Mary's lifetime the Baghdadi Jewish community that had developed a series of strongholds from India to Shanghai began to reconstitute itself in the Western world. The third portrait is of my mother, Flower. She experienced a double transition, her own and India's. Flower grew up in colonial India, witnessed India's struggle for independence during her formative teenage years and lived her middle years in an independent India. She was among the first generation of women in the Baghdadi Jewish community of Calcutta to step out of her narrowly circumscribed Jewish world. In the decade after India's independence many Jews left Calcutta, making it increasingly difficult to sustain Jewish community life. Many in Flower's generation felt compelled to come to terms with national processes within India and outside. Through the act of emigration they bridged the Baghdadi Jewish experience from the Eastern diaspora to the Western world.

The last sketch is my own. It extends and closes the lines drawn in the previous portraits. During my childhood in Calcutta the community was fast waning. I grew up in a cosmopolitan and Indian world, rather than a Baghdadi Jewish one. On leaving India to study abroad I identified as part of another diaspora—the South Asian intellectual and professional diaspora in the United States. Although I maintain tenuous ties with the Baghdadi Jewish diaspora community through my mother and through this act of writing, I am not part of the diaspora to which my forefathers and mothers belonged.

Indian and Jewish historical and social accounts omit the lives of the women I portray. These gendered and very personal accounts from a community that 'dwelled in travelling' enables the lives and voices of women that have never been heard or critically understood, to emerge. This account demanded an exploration of the categories of 'Jewishness' and 'Indianness' as well as an illustration of the significance of these particular terms to the women in each succeeding generation. Whereas Farha and Miriam only identified with Judaism, my mother and I embraced several different identities. In four generations we have variously identified ourselves as Baghdadi Jews, as British subjects, as Indians, as Israelis, and as Americans. The only identity maintained throughout the four generations was a Jewish identity. Yet what it meant to be Jewish differed considerably among us.

Judaism, as a religious practice and a way of life, structured Farha's and Miriam's worlds. Judaism is more a cultural identity for my mother and me. My grandmother and great-grandmother were deeply religious— from the early morning prayer till their *shema* (first word of the Shema Israel prayer) at night, Judaism defined their every day. They followed the letter of the law and observed rituals, customs, and festivals scrupulously. Their worlds were totally Jewish no matter where they were. My mother, who grew up in this world, knows Jewish rituals and traditions well. Unlike her foremothers, however, she selects certain aspects of traditions to observe. She is comfortable in and out of Jewish worlds and is simultaneously a part of several communities and nations.

I am Indian and Jewish and now an American citizen. I was born and brought up in Calcutta, studied in the United States during my college years, married a Bengali Hindu and now live and work in Iowa City. My mother, Flower, who lives with us now, presides over a seder in our home each year. I share this occasion with family and friends as we perform a not so serious and selective reading of the Hagadah. An orange purposefully sits on the seder plate to remind us that a learned rabbi once said that a woman on the bima (pulpit) is as incongruous as an orange on the seder platter. I identify with some Jewish values and I acknowledge my Jewish heritage through a few gestures and symbols. My grandmother and great grandmother would not recognize my life as Jewish and would be saddened by this knowledge.

All four of us have travelled extensively and lived in many different parts of the world. By chronicling their travels we learn more about who was travelling, and for what purposes travel was undertaken by women living in diaspora communities in 'Jewish Asia'. The portraits that follow reveal how each woman drew on multiple cultural traditions—Jewish, Middle-Eastern, British, American, and Indian—without losing a sense of who they were. Because they travelled and lived as part of a community, their experience was not one of displacement. To be part of a diaspora and not rooted in one place is distinct from being 'displaced', which suggests that one is out of place and disoriented or disconnected from community. The Baghdadi community rooted its members and provided them with a sense of place in diverse settings.

This set of stories engages a range of issues of interest to contemporary scholarship. The stories challenge the dominant paradigms through which the colonial experience has been presented. They enable us to go beyond conceptualizing this experience only through the categories of colonizer or colonized. These women's lives, lying between British and local cultures, show how a broader range of actors were implicated and impacted upon differently by the colonial experience. The travel experiences of the women in this diaspora community depict what it meant to dwell in travelling, sundering the binary polarization between 'travel' and 'dwelling'. Issues of identity—both personal and community—are central to each of the narratives. These accounts underline the fluidity and the political nature of identity constructions, challenging essentialist identity claims.

In this telling I am an insider, a daughter of the Baghdadi Jewish community, yet more often feel like an outsider. I look back into a world I knew as a child: a world that no longer exists in Calcutta except in shadows, musty rooms, and the old, lined faces animated only by their memories. When I travel to visit relatives in Calcutta, London, and Tel Aviv, I tread familiar ground and encounter the past fleetingly. Childhood memories echo in the voices, accents, and gestures of my aunts and uncles. My relatives are eager to talk about the good times they had in Calcutta. They tell old stories over and over. They recall names of family members, friends, and servants who are no longer a part of their lives. My aunts remind me to be sure to taste the *aloo makallahs*—a Calcutta Jewish potato delicacy. The famed potatoes are deep fried till they are a golden brown. They are crisp on the outside and almost hollow and very soft on the inside. My uncles explain that the *aloos* have been specially prepared. So many times I am told how, after many trials and errors, the right kind of potatoes had been found to make this speciality. The other guests on such occasions tell the hostess how perfectly the *aloos* have been cooked. The ultimate and awaited compliment is paid—'these taste just like they used to in Calcutta.' In this way memory is performed and community enacted.

Back in Calcutta I deliberately walk through what were once Jewish neighbourhoods. The places where the Jews lived are almost obscured by a cacophony of sounds, a medley of colours, and pungent smells. Stalls and vendors hawking colourful bolts of fabric, kurtas, export rejects, bangles and bindis dominate the landscape. Hand-pulled rickshaws, motorbikes, cars, and human and animal traffic clog the narrow lanes and encroach noisily on what were once wide thresholds and generous compounds. Behind the bustle I now notice the buildings in which they lived that I overlooked before. I stop and gaze at the spacious rooms and high ceilings behind the walls. Large windows and dilapidated wooden shutters cannot keep out the din from the streets below. For a fleeting moment I hear familiar voices calling across the street to greet and chat with one another as their children spin tops and fly kites on wide streets that double as playgrounds. I venture to and beyond the community—its members and material spaces— to talk with people whose lives intersected with the Jews in Calcutta. I learn more about popular culture, global politics and interconnected histories, such as Australian emigration policies after World War II.

Undertaking this project has made me deeply aware of who I am. I have connected with and discovered a part of myself that I barely knew, and to which I certainly never paid any serious attention. Immersed in and committed to my 'Indianness', my socialist politics, and my feminism, I ignored my Iraqi Jewish heritage. After a long lapse, this work brings my heritage back into sharp focus and into full view. In this series of family portraits I have painted the present upon the past, filling out and extending the faintly etched outlines, and imparting new meanings to a series of portraits traced long ago. The past is a part of my present and future.

There is yet another dimension to this telling. This is a collaborative narrative, undertaken in dialogue with my mother. Indeed, this book at once blends together my consciousness with my mother's, making it impossible for me sometimes to separate one from the other. I began each portrait by asking my mother to tell me what she thought was most significant about each character and the time in which she lived. My mother would tell me:

Dadi Farha was a great cook and cut an imposing figure. My mother, Miriam, was always rigid. I excelled in school and topped the high school examination.

She provided a series of dates and notes on the various members of the family, and described their personalities. Starting from her telling and cursory notes, I probed and pushed myself and her, moving each account in very different directions. Flower, who knew each of the women in this account intimately, gives me a fragile gift, sharing with me her knowledge and understanding. And now I am passing this gift of knowing, quite transformed, down the generations to my children and their children, and to the world outside. My extended family—from those two generations older than me to my siblings and cousins who live all over the world—have eagerly read what I have written. They have offered me many suggestions and corrections—their versions of these lives; together we re-create a consciousness of our history.

A part of, yet apart from, my foremothers, I do not feel overwhelmed with the angst of feminist scholars who worry as they write about 'the other' from places of privilege. While privileged, indeed, I approach these portraits somewhat as an insider and in doing so I destabilize definitions of otherness. In the words of Trinh T. Min-ha, I moved from this 'undetermined threshold where I am at once [looking] in from the outside while also looking out from the inside.' In this way I move beyond the family ties that bind me and undercut the 'inside/outside opposition.'³ I am not in the awkward position of 'seeking out intimacy and friendship with subjects on whose backs, ultimately, the books will be written.'⁴ I do not approach my mother and foremothers from the position of 'other', for I am part of them. Feelings of belonging and love imbue these pages bridging and battling the differences and distances between us.

My mother and I cast an indelible colour on this project—we are the filters through which the other lives we describe are viewed and presented. Not unexpectedly, therefore, I found it particularly hard to distance myself from my mother, especially when writing her account. I know I cannot produce an 'objective' account of her life and time, so I decided it would be best to let her speak for herself as much as possible and to let readers draw their own conclusions. Sometimes the reader may find it hard to separate her account from mine, which may lead them to think that I may share all of her views and attitudes. Despite this danger, I think it is important for her to tell her own story in her own words as much as possible. While she presents her own story in dialogue with me, she remains at the centre of her chapter. I intervene to analyse and comment on aspects of her life that enable me to elaborate upon the key themes of this book. Thus this book is at once a scholarly and family endeavour.

At times the portraits seemed to take on a life of their own. I experienced moments of uncertainty and sometimes felt I would not be able to do justice to their lives. There were a few ethically fraught moments as well. One such moment came when I telephoned my great-aunt, Ruby, Farha's daughter, in London. While delighted to hear from me, when I told her that I was writing a paper about her mother and wanted to ask her some questions, she was very reticent. She only provided perfunctory and evasive answers to my insistent and perhaps too direct questions. Aunty Ruby worried that I might write about things that could upset her mother, though she has been dead almost fifty years. She told me: 'Darling, why do you want to stir up the past? What is past is past. Let the dead rest in peace. Why disturb her now after all these years?' Aunty Ruby's relationship to memory is fundamentally different from mine. Whereas my cosmology of memory encourages me to stir up the past, she is loath to do so. So, despite Aunty Ruby's entreaties, I felt compelled to go on with this project and was motivated to do so by several family members. I did my best to reassure Aunty Ruby that I would not dishonour or disturb her mother. Later that year when I visited Ruby in her small sheltered apartment in London, I gave her the chapter I wrote about her mother, Farha. When I visited her again the following day, Aunty Ruby asked me a few questions that indirectly told me that she had read my work. I interpreted this to mean that, after seeing what I had written, she had no major objections but did not want to discuss or dwell on it further.

My telling has been superimposed on my mother's telling; my great-aunt Ruby's silences lurk just beneath the surface. This is a multilayered telling grounded in family mythology, remembering, and forgetting. I have conceived the three major narratives of my foremothers as life histories that I tell knowing full well that my telling is coloured by my own perceptions, inclinations, and the times. I am fully aware that in my accounts 'some memories are elaborated, some elided, some never summoned up at all',[5] making these portraits only fragments selected from the totality of their lives. Thus this account is necessarily very different from the story that my granny and great-grandmother would have told had they wanted to speak about their lives.

I have sought to cross-reference and substantiate the family narratives with historical materials, oral interviews with other members of the community, inside and outside experts and my own perceptions and experiences of growing up Jewish in Calcutta. I have visited, interviewed, and spent time with older members of the community in Calcutta, London,

New York and Tel Aviv, gathering impressions of relatives and friends who knew and cared about the culture and the women whose lives I portray. I have listened carefully to their words, as well as their silences. Each time, as we talk with each other my eyes wander around the familiar, worn furnishings. Sometimes I scribble a few notes. Mostly I strive to get a sense of what is important to them, a sense of how they viewed my granny and my great-grandmother, how they remember their own past and view their present and future. They tell me that they are so happy that I came to see them. I remind them of my mother. They want me to come again and tell me that they will cook special dishes for me. They ask after my mother and send her their love. They are now old and frail. When they pass away, an entire century and a half of Jewish life in Calcutta, from women's perspectives, will be irretrievable. If I do not tell the stories of the women in my family now, they will be lost forever.

Notes

Flyleaf: Women making matzahs in Calcutta.

1 Lila Abu-Lughod in *Writing Women's Worlds: Bedouin Stories* (Berkeley: University of California Press, 1993) speaks of this as writing against culture.

2 Meredith Tax, 'The Power of the Word' in Jael Silliman and Ynestra King (eds.), *Dangerous Intersections: Feminist Perspectives on Population, Environment and Development* (Cambridge, MA: South End Press, 1999), p. 113.

3 Trinh T. Min-ha, 'Not You/Like You: Post-Colonial Women and the Interlocking Question of Identity and Difference,' in Gloria Anzaldua (ed.), *Making Face, Making Soul: Creative and Critical Perspectives by Feminists of Color* (San Francisco: Aunt Lute Books, 1990), pp. 371-5.

4 Ruth Behar, *Translated Woman* (Boston: Beacon Press, 1993), p. 297.

5 Kamla Bhasin and Ritu Menon, *Borders and Boundaries: Women in India's Partition* (New Delhi: Kali for Women, 1998), p. 18. They discuss the ways in which women traumatized by the Partition remember their experiences, and the necessarily incomplete nature of the stories they recount. While aware of this incompleteness the authors stress the value of listening to their memories and incorporating their versions of the events they witnessed into our understanding of that particular moment in history.

Introduction:

Indian and Colonial Frames

$\mathcal{I}$N THE EIGHTEENTH, NINETEENTH, AND TWENTIETH CENTURIES, the Baghdadi Jewish diaspora stretched from Baghdad to Shanghai and westwards to London. This Middle Eastern trading diaspora community is strikingly different from other Middle Eastern Jewish communities and the European Jewish diaspora, which is considered the quintessential diaspora. This privileged trading community demonstrates the need to draw distinctions between Jewish diasporas and underlines the point that the Jewish experience cannot be generalized. The lives of each of the women described in this book unequivocally suggest that diaspora movements can be understood as historic processes through which community members have flourished and do not have to be overwhelmingly conceived in terms of communities experiencing loss. Borrowing a term from Arjun Appadurai's work, I frame this diaspora as a 'diaspora of hope.'[1]

Narrating the history and experiences of this diaspora community from the vantage point of Calcutta, the nerve centre of the British Empire, contextualizes this diaspora in relation to processes of empire and nation building. The time frame of this narrative enables an examination of the ways in which members of this minority diasporic community, and the community as a unit, responded and adapted to both colonialism and decolonization. It highlights the particular roles that minority communities play in colonial and national processes, inviting us to rethink not only standard discourses of these historical processes but also notions of personal, communal and national identity formation.

Responding to new economic impulses generated by colonialism, the Baghdadi Jewish trading community extended and elaborated ancient and medieval mercantile routes. For centuries these trading networks connected ports on different oceans and continents, producing distinct cultures along the routes that interacted with and related to one another for centuries. During the colonial period, port cities like Calcutta, Rangoon, and Shanghai were cosmopolitan and outward looking, and often differed markedly from places in the interior of the land masses on which they were situated. Communities in these connecting ports were integrated by the sea and often had more dealings and shared a more common culture with one another than with their respective interiors.

'Jewish Asia', of which the Baghdadi Jews were a part, was culturally much like the 'Black Atlantic' and the 'medieval Jewish Mediterranean.'[2] Throughout 'Jewish Asia', small communities of Baghdadi Jews carried out their business ventures and community life in key financial and port cities. Calcutta, because of the ambitions of Portuguese and then British traders, became a significant point on this circuit. Traders from many parts of the world, including Armenians, Greeks, Portuguese, and Baghdadi Jews, were drawn to this colonial port city. In the eighteenth century Calcutta became an important 'contact zone',[3] in which imperial and local cultures sometimes clashed and sometimes merged to produce new cultural and social forms.

The Baghdadi Jewish diaspora is best conceived as an interconnected web of relationships sustained over spaces but not contained by any one place. Feminist geographers like Doreen Massey have extended the idea of oceans connecting people and cultures to look at space in terms of social processes. She notes: 'The particular mix of social relations which are thus part of what defines a uniqueness of any place is by no means included within the space itself. Importantly, it includes relations which stretch beyond—the global as part of what constitutes the local, the outside as part of the inside. . .' Reconceptualizing space in terms of social relations, and underlining the point that the identities of places are 'always unfixed, contested and multiple' captures the dynamic qualities of space and the notion that space cannot be contained within a geographical site.[4] Thus, while Calcutta is a focal point in which the stories of the individuals and the community unfold, the city does not contain them. The Baghdadi Jews of Calcutta depended on other Jews in Basra, Rangoon, Bombay, Karachi, Singapore and Shanghai for religious, financial, and social support. These scattered, small, interdependent communities were part of a much wider 'imagined community',[5] to use Benedict Anderson's much-used term.

Above View of Writer's Buildings.

This 'imagined community' provided the business links as well as the cultural and religious resources the Baghdadi Jews in the port cities needed to sustain themselves. It was not only goods and traders that moved through this circuit. Women moved from one community to another in search of marriage partners, and entire families moved to be part of family celebrations: weddings, brits (circumcisions), or bar mitzvahs. Families also travelled to be with each other in times of need and for extended visits. Marriages, commercial news, business, and family connections welded the small communities of Baghdadi Jews into an important economic and cultural presence in the East. Travellers and religious envoys who moved back and forth across the diaspora were reassuring, living evidence that members of these scattered communities were indeed connected to one another.

It is more accurate to view the Baghdadi Jewish diaspora as a multi-centred circuit, rather than conceptualizing Baghdad as being at the core and Calcutta or Shanghai on the periphery of this complex circuit. For instance, while these communities looked to Baghdad for religious inspiration and leadership, the community's vigour and economic muscle was flexed in places like Bombay, Calcutta, and Shanghai. These commercial port cities supported the Jewish community in Iraq and provided economic opportunities for Jews in their times of need, as for example during the Second World War, when Jewish families of Calcutta provided refuge for many European Jews fleeing the Holocaust as well as their relatives who trekked into Calcutta from Burma. This 'multi-centred' diaspora network, like the medieval Jewish Mediterranean diaspora of which it was an extension, was commercially self-sustaining. The Baghdadi Jews of this diaspora were able to successfully adopt and adapt diverse cultural traditions to an essentially Sephardic core.

This Baghdadi trading diaspora flourished under colonial rule. When the first Baghdadi Jewish settler, Shalome Cohen, arrived in Calcutta in the late eighteenth century, the British had identified Calcutta as an important commercial centre. Its appeal was enhanced by its connection to both river and ocean traffic. Beginning in 1853 the British constructed a railroad to connect Calcutta with other strategic military and trading locations. The British established the key economic institutions, such as the imperious Customs House, the stately Stock Exchange, the commercial banks, and later the railroads, which were essential for trade to flourish in Calcutta. These economic and bureaucratic structures facilitated trade, while the

ramparts of Fort William on the banks of the River Hooghly afforded
Calcutta's merchants political protection and security in their business
enterprises. Calcutta was close to many important raw materials—silks and
muslins from Dacca, as well as the cash crops that grew in the rural areas
of Bengal and Bihar. Sesame oil, jute, cotton goods, sugar, spices, indigo,
and lac were all shipped out through the port of Calcutta to Eastern and
Western destinations. Indian historians have noted how the riches of the
whole of eastern India were plundered and exported to Europe through
Calcutta. According to Pradip Sinha's Marxist analysis Calcutta 'grew as a
typically colonial city, linking the hinterland of primary production with
the plantation and mining enclaves, and exporting the entire product (as
well as providing the services involved) in the interests of an externally ori-
ented imperial economy.'[6] The Baghdadi Jewish merchants of Calcutta
played a role in these colonial processes. They had stakes in many plantation and primary products and facilitated these extractive and exploitative
forces. Jewish traders competed with other trading communities, especially the Armenians and the Parsis, in this phase of mercantile capitalism.

Baghdadi Jewish merchants of Calcutta made large fortunes in the
opium trade in the first part of the nineteenth century. In his authoritative
account of the Calcutta Jewish community, Rabbi Ezekiel Musleah notes
the role of the Jews in the opium trade:

> The opium trade was dominated by Jews. The Indian farmer sold
> all his produce to the British Government of India, which auc-
> tioned it to the highest bidder, to the value of five or six million
> rupees annually. Then it was exported privately to Penang, Hong
> Kong, Shanghai and Singapore mainly in Chinese boats. Even the
> shipping of opium was almost entirely in Jewish hands. In January
> 1888, for example, 4546 chests were exported, 2870 being
> through Jewish merchants.[7]

Musleah's detailed records of Jewish economic interests are invaluable,
but he does not place them in the broader context of British imperial interests that linked distant parts of the world in a series of exploitative relationships. More recently, Thomas Timberg has mapped the economic connections between the various British commercial endeavours that upheld
and advanced the imperial project:

> The opium produced in India was exchanged for tea in China
> which, in turn was shipped to England to permit India to pay for

its imports from England and for the services of the Englishmen who ruled it. Many of the leading fortunes of all communities in nineteenth-century India were made in this opium trade.[8]

The Baghdadi Jews played a pivotal role in this infamous and unfair triangular trade that impoverished China and India. These cash crops enriched Jewish traders and directly supported British economic hegemony and imperial rule. When the opium trade declined and was banned by the British in the early twentieth century, Jewish traders invested in cotton and jute products as export staples. Another source of fabulous wealth for the Jews was indigo cultivation, sales, and shipping. For example, my father's family had indigo plantations in Gorakhpur, Bihar. Jewish traders also manufactured and exported silk, woollen, and cotton products, and dealt in precious stones.

From the nineteenth century onwards Baghdadi Jews were very involved in Calcutta's booming real estate business. By the latter half of the nineteenth century, David Joseph Ezra, a prominent Calcutta Jew, was one of the leading property owners in the city.[9] The Ezras owned some of the city's most imposing buildings in the most prestigious neighbourhoods. These include Esplanade Mansions, Ezra Mansions, and Chowringhee Mansions. All these stately buildings were built by cheap local labour. In addition to real estate, the Jews dominated other economic engines. My father's family was one of the founders of the Calcutta Stock Exchange (my father reminds me that his seat is about one hundred and twenty-five years old).[10] Thus the Baghdadi Jews, including many in my father's line, played an essential role in the development of mercantile capitalism in the colonial period in India.

When the Baghdadi Jews came to India during British colonial rule at the end of the eighteenth century, with pre-capitalist trading networks already in place, they were poised to succeed in the mercantile phase of capitalism. Baghdadi Jews had long been part of trading networks; British imperialism provided the conditions for the expansion of these networks to new areas of the world. As Timberg has noted, these networks operated as ancillary to British trading networks from at least the mid-nineteenth century onward and played an important part in India's economy.[11] Thus, a string of Baghdadi Jewish communities thrived on the underside of the colonial enterprise.

The ambivalent position of Baghdadi Jews in the colonial structure worked to their advantage. They were neither Indian nor Western, brown nor White, but sandwiched between the two, at once insiders and outsiders. They partnered both European and Indian commercial interests. As business flourished, some of the wealthier Jews transferred their business headquarters and moved to England, though the more conservative elite made Calcutta their base.

The Baghdadi Jews' relationship with India was complicated. They played an exploitative role as outsiders in the economic colonization of India, while facilitating the colonial project from the inside. They were loyal to, but never considered themselves, British—nor were they so regarded by the colonial powers. They clamoured unsuccessfully for European status, which the British never granted them. Despite their Anglicization, even the elite 'did not quite belong in the caste-ridden society of Anglo India.'[12] Most Baghdadi Jews had British colonial ideas about race and placed themselves in the upper echelons of the racial pyramid that structured social life in the colonies. Neither British nor Indian, the Baghdadi Jews clung tenaciously to their Jewish identity. While their political allegiances changed over time, their commitment to Judaism as both cultural and religious practice was central to their sense of who they were.

As a religious minority, they were always worried about assimilation. They emphasized their foreign origin and their religion to distinguish themselves from the dominant Hindu and also the minority Muslim and Christian communities. Thus, while the elites of all communities tended to mix more freely, the majority of the Baghdadi Jews lived socially in their small Jewish world and mixed neither with the Europeans nor the Indians. They had good social relations with their Indian and British counterparts but maintained their cultural and religious differences rigidly. Intermarriages were extremely rare and frowned upon. The majority of Jews went to Jewish schools and community events. This social segregation was commonplace in the Indian and colonial environment of the nineteenth and twentieth centuries, where the compartmentalization of difference was pervasive among all communities.

By the twentieth century, the majority of the Baghdadi Jews who were born in India spoke English as their primary language at school and home, Arabic to the older members of the community, and Hindustani with domestic help and in the street. They read their prayers in Hebrew but did not understand much of the language. They listened to Western music, many played the piano, and the younger folk enjoyed contemporary American dancing, which they picked up through the movies. The men went to social clubs and many enjoyed the horse races and gambling at the racecourse. They played cards, and enjoyed watching and playing cricket as well as other sports. Both men and women were exposed to the West through movies and books.

In the twentieth century wealthy and affluent Jews sent their sons to study in England, and some sent their daughters to finishing schools in Europe. The elite could afford to travel to Europe and kept in touch with English and European styles. The middle-class in the community, which constituted the majority, mimicked the elite mercantile members of the community and copied British tastes as best they could afford. Jewish homes had Western furnishings and decor: heavy mahogany and teak almirahs or cupboards, carved tables and chairs and wood and glass china cabinets for their bric-a-brac. Many of the items they used were imported from England, a common practice before India's independence in 1947.

By the turn of the twentieth century, even the poorest members of the community had adopted a Judeo-British identity. They sent their children to the Jewish schools that were run on British lines. This Anglo orientation was common among other minority communities and among many Indians. Tanya Luhrmann, in her recent study of the Parsi community, perhaps the most Anglicized community in India, comments extensively on Parsi desires to be 'as-if Englishmen'. She describes how this 'colonial native elite' shaped their ideals and sensibilities according to colonial culture—its literature, sporting and athletic ethos, pianos, and styles of dress. Luhrmann discusses the agony of coming to terms with India after independence and the difficulty of accepting the hollowness of the colonial promise:

> Still, the great promise of the white man's curtained power was that it seemed to have a threshold over which the educated, the well-born, and the successful could pass. And because of this implied advantage, those who saw themselves as the most eligible were perhaps less likely to see the invisible barriers of racial differences . . . more prone to dream of the just achievements of their desire to be 'as-if' Englishmen, for it is not too unnatural to see the world in the way that seems to suit you best.[13]

The Baghdadi Jews, like the Parsis, were loyal British subjects and fervently believed in the moral right of British rule and the colonial project that privileged them. To them Britain was the agent of progress.

Over two centuries of colonial presence in Calcutta had a deep impact on the city and the numerous communities that lived there. By the mid-twentieth century the British presence was ubiquitous—embodied in street names, colonial monuments, stone mansions, and in the Indian English spoken everywhere. British products flooded Calcutta's markets and many English men and women lived in the city. 'British' values and practices determined the way in which businesses were conducted, institutions run, sports played, and social life structured. According to Luhrmann, elite Indians, including Calcutta Jews '. . . shaped their ideals and sensibilities and the ideals and sensibilities of their children upon the canons of English colonial culture; its literature, its sociability, its competitive athletics, its pianos and lace and fitted suits.'[14] Ashis Nandy makes the important point that colonialism 'never seems to end with formal political freedom' because 'its sources lie deep in the minds of the ruler and the ruled.'[15]

Indian independence represented a moment of crisis for the Baghdadi Jewish community. Baghdadi Jews had to redefine themselves as individuals and as a community in relation to the newly forming state. Questions of their ethnic and communal identity became urgent, and they could no longer define themselves in terms of their Jewishness alone. The issues of ethnic and communal identity played out very differently than they did for more mainstream communities and for larger minority communities that had a more clearly articulated political position in the emerging nation. Diaspora communities like the Jews, because of their religious identity, economic status, and connections to Jews elsewhere, along with their colour privilege and ambiguous identity, had more options about whether to stay in India or relocate to other places. Their multiple privileges and the security that they could rely on in the new India complicate familiar stories of Jews elsewhere. The story of those Baghdadi Jews who opted to stay on in Calcutta and become part of the new nation challenges the notion of the Jew always being excluded. Thus, this diasporic experience undercuts easy generalizations about the situation of Jews and of members of diasporas being necessarily disadvantaged and especially vulnerable.

In the first decade after India's independence, idealism, exhilaration, tension and pain were equally inscribed in the process of transition from a colonial to a postcolonial world. India and the Baghdadi Jews who remained in India after independence were engaged likewise in this process of deforming/reforming their identity. Arjun Appadurai captures the constant negotiations that have to be made in the decolonization process:

> For the former colony, decolonization is a dialogue with the colonial past, and not a simple dismantling of colonial habits and modes of life . . . In the Indian case, the cultural aspects of decolonization affect every domain of public life . . . In every major public debate in contemporary India, one underlying strand is always the question of what to do with the shreds and patches of the colonial heritage. Some of these patches are institutional; others are ideological and aesthetic.[16]

The Baghdadi Jews of Calcutta responded to the increased possibilities for immigration to Australia, England, and other Commonwealth countries in the forties and fifties. The West had enormous glamour and appeal as a place of opportunity and advancement and so lured many Jews away from Calcutta. Once a few Jews started leaving, others quickly followed, as this was a tight-knit community. Thus in less than a decade there was no longer the critical mass left in Calcutta to sustain community life. Those who stayed on faced no economic or professional disadvantages but felt nostalgia for a way of life that was lost. They missed being part of a community and many felt left behind.

The Jewish exodus from Calcutta was propelled by the War, Indian independence, and the formation of Israel. A number of the younger members of the Jewish community believed that emigration would improve their economic and professional prospects. A wave of young people, after settling themselves in London in fairly good professional positions, sent for their extended families, while other members of the community emigrated to Australia, Canada, and the United States. This rapid movement of people destabilized and unsettled the community. In a short span of five years the community lost so many members that some basic Jewish services, such as having a mohel to perform the ritual circumcision, were no longer available. Over the next decade the community infrastructure crumbled.

The Calcutta Jews left only a few traces. There are three impressive and large synagogues, two small prayer halls, two schools (the Jewish Girls' School and Talmud Torah), and a cemetery in Narkeldanga. There are some mansions and a hospital that were owned or endowed by Jews that still bear Jewish names—the Ezra Hospital and Ezra Mansions. There are two stately buildings in the zoo—the birdhouse and the reptile house, that are named the Ezra and the Gubbay building. Ezra Street and Synagogue Street kept these names for decades. The Jewish presence has been written over by contemporary India and is only visible to those in search of it.

A handful of wealthy Jews still have their homes in south Calcutta. Although some of these older community members would return fairly regularly to be taken care of by old retainers in familiar and comforting surroundings, they come less and less frequently. When they do, their homes are filled with the smells of Jewish cooking. A coolie from Nahoums, the popular Jewish-owned confectionery in New Market, still delivers special orders of Baghdadi delicacies like *samboosas*. Locked doors and shuttered windows are temporarily opened to the sun as elderly Jews relax in easy chairs on their verandahs. Their immediate surroundings have barely changed. Mostly they have no desire to explore the world beyond the compound and the few Jewish friends left—the world outside was alien and unfamiliar even when they lived in Calcutta.

A few of the younger folks—the children and grandchildren of Calcutta Jews—come back to discover their roots. They need permission to visit the immaculately maintained Maghen David and Beth-el synagogues that are otherwise locked behind massive iron grill gates. The caretakers of the synagogue eagerly show the visitors around. The stately columns, the patterned tiles, the heavily encrusted, silver-and-wood enclosed sefer torahs speak of a thriving past. A few visitors are keen to go beyond the community to discover India, a country of which they were a part but did not know, for throughout their sojourn they remained as Jews in India rather than being Indian Jews. Most do not come back even to visit, for they and their children have adopted numerous national identities as they merged in new hostlands and in the process lost their connection with Jewish Calcutta.

Notes

Flyleaf: A view of Lindsay Street, with New Market on the right.

1 This term has been coined by Arjun Appadurai, who also refers to 'diasporas of terror' and 'diasporas of despair' that exist in the contemporary world. See Arjun Appadurai, *Modernity at Large: Cultural Dimensions of Globalization* (Minneapolis: Minnesota University Press,1996), p. 6

2 See Paul Gilroy, *The Black Atlantic: Modernity and Double Consciousness* (Cambridge, MA: Harvard University Press, 1993), as well as the notion of the medieval Jewish Mediterranean discussed by James Clifford in *Routes: Travel and Translation in the Late Twentieth Century* (Cambridge, MA: Harvard University Press, 1997).

3 Here I am drawing on the phrase coined and defined by Mary Louise Pratt in *Imperial Eyes: Travel Writing and Transculturation* (London: Routledge, 1992).

4 Doreen Massey, *Space, Place and Gender* (Minneapolis: University of Minnesota Press, 1994), p. 5. This insight negates the notion that culture can be a bounded entity. She pays particular attention to definitions of space that are not physically contained.

5 Benedict Anderson, *Imagined Communities* (London: Verso, 1991).

6 Pradip Sinha, 'Calcutta and the Currents of History 1690–1912' in Sukanta Chaudhuri (ed.), *Calcutta the Living City: Volume 1: The Past.* (Calcutta: Oxford University Press, 1990), p. 32.

7 Ezekiel Musleah, *On the Banks of the Ganga: The Sojourn of the Jews in Calcutta* (North Quincy, MA: Christopher Publishing House, 1975), p. 46. Rabbi Musleah, who has written one of the key texts on the Calcutta Jewish community, is a member of the community and served as a rabbi in Calcutta in the mid-twentieth century. Today he lives in Philadelphia.

8 Thomas A. Timberg, 'Indigenous and Non-Indigenous Jews' in Nathan Katz (ed.), *Studies of Indian Jewish Identity* (New Delhi: Manohar Publishers and Distributors, 1995), p. 138.

9 Musleah, *On the Banks of the Ganges*, p. 54. While the Jews owned some of the most valuable real estate in the city, as did the Armenians, the Europeans had no interest in the land market as they did not plan to live on in India after making their fortunes.

10 Aaron Obadiah Cohen was one of the founders of the Calcutta Stock Exchange.

11 Timberg in Katz, *Studies of Indian Jewish Identity,* p. 137.

12 Ibid., p. 141.

13 Tanya M. Luhrmann, *The Good Parsi: The Fate of a Colonial Elite in a Postcolonial Society* (Cambridge, MA: Harvard University Press, 1996), p. 4.

14 Luhrmann speaking about elite Indians with particular reference to Parsis in *The Good Parsi*, p. 9.

15 See Ashis Nandy, *The Intimate Enemy: Loss and Recovery of Self under Colonialism* (Delhi: Oxford University Press, 1983), p. 3.

16 Appadurai, 'Playing With Modernity: The Decolonization of Indian Cricket' in *Modernity at Large*, p. 89.

Farha:
Crossing Borders, Maintaining Boundaries

$\mathcal{F}$ARHA, MY MOTHER TELLS ME, 'was sent by ship on her own volition to marry a man thirty-five years older, that could have been her father. Her husband-to-be, Saleh, dutifully met her at the dockside in Kidderpore in Calcutta where a formal kiddushim (pre-nuptial agreement) was performed. He brought her a full set of clothing. In her new finery she was escorted, well-chaperoned, to be married a week later to this tall, handsome man.' This is my mother's rendition of what her dadi (father's mother in Urdu) told her. When Flower asked Farha, by then an old woman, how she felt about marrying a man so much older, she said: 'I never regretted it. I was pampered and treated like a queen by him. I never regarded him as an older man as he was so young and strong all his life. I would do it all over again.' Farha's tender feelings and great love for Saleh were reciprocated. Older family members spoke of how Saleh adored and respected his young wife.

Farha, my great-grandmother, was born in Baghdad into the well-established, landed, Musree family. She was the only daughter of Yusef Musree. Yusef arranged for Farha to marry Saleh Baqaal Abraham, a small-scale trader based in Calcutta who left Baghdad as a young man to seek his fortune in India. A wave of Jews had originally fled from Baghdad when they were persecuted by Daud Pasha (1817-31), as did some Meshed Jews who were being forcibly converted in Persia (1839). They had prospered in India and stories of their commercial success and business opportunities enticed other Jews like Saleh to seek their fortunes there. Saleh arrived at Calcutta sometime in the mid-1860s, at the high point of British imperialism in India. (In 1858 the East India Company had transferred its rule to the British Crown.) Farha joined Saleh some thirty years later.

The British favoured the Jews, as they did other minorities who were too small in number to pose a threat to their supremacy. Elite members of the Baghdadi Jewish community especially benefited from colonial rule, which opened up great commercial futures for them. Influential families like the Sassoons of Bombay and the Gubbays, Ezras, and Eliases from Calcutta traded across the Middle East and Asia on a large scale and sought to identify with their British overlords. Thus, a few elite Baghdadi families moved rather quickly from their status as 'alien pioneers' to become key commercial interlocutors for the British. The Baqaals, my maternal ancestors, did not belong in this category. Small-scale traders like Saleh had minimal interactions with colonial authorities and institutions, and virtually no social interactions with the British. Although the structure of the economy was determined by colonial rule, they were not as aligned to British political and commercial interests as were the Jewish trading elite who interacted with the British in social and business spheres in India, England, and in the various eastern trading ports of the Empire.[1]

Saleh selected Calcutta, the capital of colonial India and the second city of the Empire, as his business base.[2] Eighteenth-century Calcutta was organized around three distinct areas—a small European town (White town) built around Fort William, an intermediate town (Grey town), and a large Indian area (Black town) to the north. Pradip Sinha describes the White town as 'an artefact of planning and high level real estate development' and an 'exemplary artefact of colonial settlement.'[3] Sinha's and other accounts portray the Indian or Black town as a teeming settlement with a mixed crowd of people. Its original nucleus was the Burrabazaar (Great Market), which expanded from a yarn and textile market into a huge wholesale market. The Grey town was cosmopolitan and spilled over into the Black town. While each of the three distinct 'towns' had its own character, they were not rigidly demarcated.

The White town featured many impressive mansions and government offices built by the British and local elite. The official buildings, concentrated in the well-laid out European section, included the stately Writer's Buildings, the New Council House, the Town Hall, the Mint, and the Senate House. Many of Calcutta's buildings featured classical and neoclassical architectural designs with a hint of Persian style and an emphasis on rich ornamentation. Between 1870 and 1905 many more imperial buildings were erected by the British and Calcutta's new indigenous and merchant elites, underscoring the city's status as a booming colonial centre of commerce and trade. The stately homes and official buildings reflected local, Middle Eastern, and European architectural traditions.[4] Despite the colonial conceit of many buildings and the wealth of local elites (foreign and indigenous), Pradip Sinha reminds us that by the time Saleh arrived the city extended over seven square miles and was basically comprised of hutments that came to be known as the great slums of Calcutta.[5]

The Jewish area, including the synagogues and schools, lay about half a mile from the bank of the Hooghly and was wedged between the White town to the south and the Black town to the north. This Grey area was home to many of the city's trading communities including Portuguese, Chinese, Armenian, Parsi, and Jewish merchants. These various ethnic communities lived cheek by jowl in an extremely limited area. Many in these merchant communities continued the peddling tradition of maritime trade. From the mid-eighteenth to the mid-nineteenth century the Persian language and culture dominated the higher echelons of this cosmopolitan enclave as well as the Indian part of town. The lower levels of society, especially in the late eighteenth century, spoke a kind of pidgin Portuguese. Dressed in Arabic clothing and fluent in Arabic, Saleh had business interests as well as cultural moorings that were predominantly located in the Grey town. The formality and style of the White town was alien to Saleh. Only a handful of wealthy Jews lived in the European area in the late nineteenth and first few decades of the twentieth century. This elite was more Anglicized than middle-class Jews like Saleh, who were decidedly Judeo-Arabic in orientation and custom.

Calcutta, a dynamic maritime centre, had a strong commercial infrastructure and the necessary religious structures to sustain a small but influential Jewish community. It already had two synagogues, the Neveh Shalome (House of Peace) and the Beth-el (House of God). All powers relating to the religious, communal, and social affairs of the community were vested in the Synagogue Committee, which served as a liaison between the Jewish community and the Government of India up until the 1880s, when the system disintegrated because of internal rivalries among community members. The Baghdadi Jewish community has been categorized as 'prosperous'; however, ironically, perhaps half of the community was poor and dependent on Jewish charities. The other half was divided between the middle class (about 35%) and the wealthy, the affluent, and the opulent.[6] Saleh Baqaal was a member of the middle classes who owned and managed small businesses and were dependent neither on the commercial enterprises of the British nor on elite Jews for their employment.

Unlike other Iraqi Jewish traders, who were called box-wallahs (literally, peddlers of merchandise from boxes), Saleh's small trading interests extended beyond India—his trading world spanned 'Jewish Asia.' Over this wide geographic space, small communities of Baghdadi Jews carried out their business ventures and community life in key financial and port cities like Calcutta, Rangoon, Penang, Singapore, Djakarta, and Shanghai. These scattered, small, interdependent communities were part of a much wider 'imagined community,' and were in constant conversation with each other, sharing a similar world and worldview even though they were not tied to any one territory or geographic place. This 'imagined community' provided both the business links and the cultural and religious resources the Baghdadi Jews in the port cities needed to sustain themselves. Marriages, commercial news, business, and family connections welded the small communities of Baghdadi Jews into an important economic and cultural presence in the East.

Saleh, very much part of this 'imagined community', travelled extensively on business between Basra and Shanghai. He brought fez caps to India and the Far East, and returned to Baghdad with silk, spices, and tea. Musree, his business partner and friend, managed the Baghdad side of the business. Soon the two partners set up a small import-export trade that extended to Bombay, Madras, Calcutta, Rangoon, Singapore, Penang, and Djakarta. By his late forties, having established himself, Saleh sought a bride. He turned to Yusef Musree to find himself a suitable match. Arranged marriages were customary in those days, and it was not unusual for a family to send a daughter off to be married in another part of this trading community. Yusef sent his fifteen-year-old daughter, Farha, to Calcutta sometime in 1894-95 to be Saleh's bride.[7] The only thing unusual about this match was that Saleh was so much older than Farha.

During the early years of their marriage, Saleh and Farha stayed with Saleh's brothers and sisters, some of whom had settled in Calcutta. It was the custom among Baghdadi Jews to live as an extended family. Saleh continued to travel on business, and, contrary to prevailing customs, his young wife accompanied him. Because he was so much older than Farha, Saleh was reluctant to leave her in Calcutta when he was away on long trips. We know that she travelled with him from the notes inscribed in Saleh's prayerbook—which has been kept in the family—at the back of which he notes the days, places and times his children were born and asks the Lord to 'keep and preserve them.'[8]

In 1896 Farha's first child, Dinah Katoon, was born in Bombay.[9] Farha's next two children, Eliyahu Hayeem (Elias), who is my grandfather, and Mazal To'be (Mozelle), were born in Singapore. Elias was born in June 1899 and Mozelle in December 1900. Farha's fourth child, Abraham, was born in Baghdad in 1903, when she returned to her home for a few years on an extended visit. Thereafter Farha returned to Calcutta, where she gave birth to three more children in 1909, 1911, and 1914.

Travel in those days was very slow—a business trip to the Far East took between six and eight months, including long halts at ports along the way. This explains why several of the Baqaal children were born en route. Elias and Mozelle were born in Jewish homes. It was considered a mitzvah (good deed) to provide home and shelter for months at a time to fellow Baghdadi Jewish visitors. Farha both extended and received this courtesy. The diaspora Jewish communities were 'a refuge, a home, a place of security in an alien world' within which the Jewish travellers could sustain their identity.[10] While Saleh ventured into the marketplaces and docks of Penang, Rangoon, and Singapore, Farha stayed within the domestic confines of the Baghdadi Jewish community. She assisted her hosts with cooking and other household chores. Although domestic servants performed many of the heavier tasks, they needed supervision for religious reasons (such as the keeping of the laws of kashrut or dietary restrictions), and this task of supervision was the responsibility of the women of the household. Living, working and chatting for extended periods of time with the women and children of these widespread households, Farha forged strong bonds with other women of this diaspora and expanded her social network.

The food Farha helped prepare during her visits to places like Rangoon, Singapore, or Penang was almost the same as that cooked at home in Basra and Calcutta. There were some variations in the recipes and spices depending on the availability of local fruits and vegetables. The rituals and customs were also familiar to her because, although the Jews across the diaspora came from various parts of the Middle East, they were Baghdadi in their cultural orientation. While food preparation took up a major part of the day, Baghdadi women also spent a great deal of time in religious and ritual activities.

The day began with the washing of the hands and the *naytilaat yaday-*

Above View of Hall and Anderson Building.
Below View of Raj Bhavan, now the Governor's residence.

im prayer. This ritual was performed using a special brass vessel with a spout. Water was poured alternately thrice on each hand. After this ritual the men read *tefiloth* at home or at the synagogue, and the women offered a similar morning prayer. Throughout the day they recited *brachot* (blessings) for each item of food they ate or liquid that passed their lips. They even recited *brachot* before drinking a glass of water. The women read *tehilim* (psalms) during the day: they were expected to read 150 psalms a month, though the more religious women read 150 psalms a week. At night the *shema* was recited aloud as they placed their cupped fingers over their faces. Their homes were run on strictly kosher lines. Elaborate preparations were undertaken for the Sabbath. Oil wicks were lit to usher in and to take leave of the Sabbath bride, for the Sabbath is welcomed as a bride in Jewish homes. The making of oil wicks was a ritual carried out by women. My mother tells me that they used thin bamboo sticks wrapped in cotton. Poorer Jewish women made and sold these wicks to the more affluent.

While the men regularly attended the synagogue, most women only went to the synagogue during the festivals and on some Sabbaths when there were bar mitzvahs or maftirs of significance to them.[11] Friday night and Saturday brunch brought special Jewish dishes to the dining table. Large families and relatives came together to eat and pray. This observance of Baghdadi traditions was very important: it created a sense of community and belonging, the familiar rhythms of Baghdadi community life helping to root them in a foreign environment.

Friendships, and strong community and family bonds made the Baghdadi Jews feel they were at home despite being in distant places. The women enjoyed each other's company, and long hours were spent sewing, making wicks, preparing food, playing games like backgammon and cards, chatting and gossiping while they worked or relaxed in the shade of their verandahs or courtyards. Iraqi Jewish women were very active in community functions and ritual events held in their homes or at the synagogue, where they performed specific roles and duties. On occasion they enjoyed family outings, picnics and community gatherings; women attended parties in the company of their friends and relatives.

Across the diaspora Farha and other middle-class Baghdadi women of her generation wore 'wrappers'. These loose cotton gowns flowed from the shoulder to the ankle, much like a kaftan, with wide gathered collars and elbow-length sleeves, often trimmed with lace. They wore a petticoat and drawers under the wrapper. Married women covered their heads with *yasmahs* (scarves) that were fastened around gathered knots of hair or knotted at the forehead. When they went outdoors, their wrappers were covered with shawls. My mother vividly recalls a beautiful black, Spanish-style, mantilla shawl that Farha wore when she was middle-aged. The shawl was probably made of pure silk and embroidered in China. Its large red roses and long silk hanging threads made for a dramatic effect.

Iraqi Jewish men in the middle and late nineteenth century also wore Arabic style clothing both at home and outside. Their clothing was loose and flowing. They wore a *dagla* (long coat), *kamsan* (long shirt), *labsan* (undershirt), and *sadaria* (outer vest). Many men also wore turbans and comfortable slippers. It was not till the turn of the century that the *dagla* gave way to the suit, the wrapper to the dress. By the early twentieth century affluent Jewish men wearing ties, suits, and buttoned-up shoes to the synagogue presented a different image from the older generations with their flowing, regal robes and elaborate slippers. Other classes of Jews followed their lead and wore Western clothing, though it was less formal. With regard to language, too, Arabic and Hindustani yielded to English.

While Anglicization was working its way into the culture of the community, the religious aspects and ritual of the community remained conservatively Middle Eastern. Baghdadi rituals and musical tunes were closely adhered to in worship. Till the mid-twentieth century the hazans (cantors) wore long white silk robes trimmed with gold for ceremonial occasions at the synagogue. An imposing stiff white head-dress enhanced their splendour. The head-dress sat snugly on the forehead and rose from a fitted rim, ending in a flat top. On Yom Kippur men wore white cloth slippers made especially for them by the Chinese shoemakers of Calcutta.

The Jewish communities across the diaspora were inward looking and self-contained. All the women Farha knew intimately or met socially in Calcutta or the other diaspora communities spoke Arabic. Like many other Baghdadi women, Farha could write in Arabic and she used the Hebrew script to do so. She read Hebrew but could not understand it—it was the language of prayer. Like other men and women she had a working knowledge of the local languages, enough to communicate with people outside the Jewish community. For instance, Farha spoke a little Hindustani and knew some English words in addition to Arabic. She spoke Hindustani to domestic help and in the streets, and a smattering of English and Hindustani to her grandchildren, who did not speak Arabic.

Speaking mostly in Arabic, wearing Middle Eastern clothing, and preparing and eating Iraqi Jewish food, Farha and the Jewish families with whom she stayed in the various diaspora communities were surrounded by people very different from them. On extended visits she heard her hosts speaking a smattering of local languages. A mere glance out of the window or an outing exposed her to a multitude of unfamiliar sights, sounds, and smells. The sights and sounds of Calcutta differed from those of Shanghai, Singapore, and Djakarta. So, whereas the reassuringly familiar interiors of Baghdadi Jewish homes in ports across this diaspora were very similar, the places where they were located were very different—unknown, foreign surroundings from which Farha and other Baghdadi Jews purposefully kept a great distance.

The Hebrew–Arabic newspapers feature numerous accounts of community members travelling for business, vacations, marriages and religious functions, despite ocean travel in the late nineteenth century being arduous. Family and business visits forged a sense of community across the diaspora; they consolidated kinship and patronage networks, enabled news to be transmitted and exchanged, and renewed, recreated, and sealed family bonds. Since the communities were so small, marriage outside the immediate local community was often essential to avoid too much inbreeding. Farha had two of her nieces, Mazal Tov and Tufahah Khatoon, sent out from Baghdad to stay with her in Calcutta for several months. As Baghdadi brides were in great demand, Farha arranged suitable matches for each of them. Mazal married Elias Nahoum of the well-established Nahoum family of Calcutta in 1914.[12] Tufahah became the bride of Saul Isaac and went to Djakarta in 1915.[13] My mother tells me that Tufahah's children emigrated in the 1930s from Djakarta to Israel, where they have prospered.[14]

By the end of the nineteenth century a great deal of the ocean travel was in small British steamships. Jews travelled frequently between Rangoon and Calcutta because these two ports were fairly close to each other. My mother tells me that entire families, complete with servants to help with the cooking on deck, travelled as 'deck passengers' to attend weddings or bar mitzvahs of relatives in Rangoon. Although deck travel was primarily for those who could not afford to pay for a cabin and meals on board, many Jewish families chose to travel this way as, due to their strict observance of kashrut, they would not eat the food prepared for the regular passengers and preferred to do their own cooking on deck. I can well imagine the scene: the servants sitting on their haunches around a chulha (clay stove) preparing the food while groups of Jewish women rolled out the bedding, chatted, and sang together—a veritable family picnic on the high seas.

Whereas Calcutta Jews most frequently travelled to Rangoon, many travelled greater distances. Sons were often sent to settle in the various port cities and trading centres to extend a family's commercial reach. Girls were often sent to another diaspora community to be married or find a suitable marriage partner. Particular prayers and rituals were performed to ensure a safe passage on the numerous journeys that were routinely undertaken. My mother recalls a ritual where a piece of the *afikomen* (the bottom of three matzahs eaten at the Passover seder) were saved and dried to a hard flat stone. This symbolic stone was saved for family members undertaking ocean travel during the year. They believed that just as God had parted the Red Sea to ensure a safe passage for the Israelites fleeing from the Egyptians, so a piece of *afikomen* tossed into a stormy sea would calm the waters and keep the voyager safe from all harm.

Although Farha travelled many miles and over many seas, the worlds in which she moved were Baghdadi Jewish worlds, so much so that her children hardly recall the fact that she travelled extensively! When I asked Aunty Ruby about the places her mother had travelled to, she could not recall any. Yet the notes in Saleh's fragile prayerbook tell us the opposite. Farha's children and grandchildren do not recall any stories of her travels, and remember no particular objects in their home or special foods that Farha prepared that spoke of the many places she had visited. Her only narrative was that of the Middle Eastern Jewish diaspora. She did not go out to see the sights as a tourist or adventurer when she visited relatives and family in various locations. The places she visited seemed to be of little interest in and of themselves—they were meaningful only as locations where family and relatives lived. Thus, whether in Calcutta, Rangoon, or Penang, Farha was part of the Baghdadi Jewish community to which she was connected through kinship or other ties. It was a familiar space surrounded by worlds she did not know, as alien as her surroundings in Calcutta were, places from which she maintained her distance.

While comfortable in their local settings, the Baghdadi Jews never identified with or saw themselves as part of the lands in which they lived.[15] Colonial practice encouraged Jews to develop a sense of distinctiveness vis-à-vis the Hindu and Muslim population. Under the British, the Indian Jews were encouraged to manifest and articulate an ethnic identity that could not be defined within the caste framework. Religious differences became the focal point in defining ethnic identity and the markers for social inter-action.[16]

Although Hindu and Muslim day servants worked in Farha's household she rarely met socially with non-Jews and knew little about non-Jewish lives and worlds. She had many Jewish neighbours, but she also had Chinese, Armenian, Anglo-Indian, and Parsi families living in close prox-imity. While the neighbours greeted each other, and their younger children played together in the compounds of the buildings in which they lived, nei-ther the adults nor the children went to each other's homes. All the social events she attended were in other Jewish homes with Jewish families, the synagogues or Jewish schools.

As Saleh grew older, he found extensive travelling difficult, so he put down roots in Calcutta. My mother and I conjecture that Saleh and Farha must have set up a home of their own somewhere in the years between 1905 and 1910, because their last four children were born in Calcutta. Probably, by the time the two elder children were of school-going age, Farha and Saleh decided not to be away for such extended periods, even though it was quite customary for children to live with aunts, uncles, and grandparents. Rivkah, their third child, was born in 1909, Yosef Rehamim in 1911, Shelome Hye in 1914, and Isaac Faroj in 1920/21 (his birth date was not recorded in Saleh's diary and therefore remains imprecise). Isaac, the youngest child was born when Saleh had reached the venerable age of seventy-nine years. Saleh's sister and her husband, who did not have chil-dren, came to live with his family during this more settled phase of his life, when he was an elderly man.

Calcutta was a good place to settle for the couple with their growing family. It offered business opportunities and religious facilities that other Jewish communities in the East could not match. For example, Musleah states that Jewish communities in places like Singapore in the mid-nine-teenth century did not have sofers (scribes) to draw up ketubahs (marriage contracts). They looked for these services in Calcutta and often sought guidance from the community in Calcutta, which was better organized and had these important services and Jewish facilities.[17] Calcutta also had good Jewish schools. Furthermore, Saleh had relatives in Calcutta to whom his family remained close all their lives. While Saleh's brothers and sister Amam settled in Calcutta, his brother-in-law and sister Farha eventually decided to emigrate to Palestine. There they endowed a small synagogue called the Aharon Baqaal Synagogue. It now serves as an Ashkenazi shul in Mea Shearim, Jerusalem.[18]

The Baqaals maintained a very religious home, for the overriding consideration in the community was religious observation and its perpetuation.[19] Saleh was devoted to Hacham Shlomo Abid Twena, who is still renowned for his great learning and spiritualism.[20] This revered preacher earned his living by selling religious items from Baghdad and Palestine, and from the ritual slaughtering of animals and birds. He also taught Hebrew and ran a small printing press primarily to publish his own religious writings. Saleh regularly attended the synagogue in Hacham Twena's home and donated a sefer torah to it. The preacher's home-cum-synagogue was at 10 Lower Chitpore Road, the poorest section of the Jewish quarter. Later Hacham Twena moved about half a mile to 3 Blackburn Lane, still in the poorer section. He preached in Arabic and conducted daily and Sabbath services from 1893 till he died in 1913. He fell out of favour with the community elders, whom he criticized for their indifference to the poor within the community. The poorer members of the community flocked to his congregation.[21] There are numerous legends about Hacham Shlomo, who is venerated today in Jerusalem and through the Sephardic world for his teachings.[22]

The homes in which the Baqaals lived were all in the old Jewish quarter which was bound by Old China Bazaar Street, Sukeas Lane, Lower Chitpore Road, and Canning Street, where three synagogues were located.[23] A description of the area states:

> In the middle of the last century . . . Lower Chitpur Road rivaled the Chandi Chowk of Delhi. Its display of hookah bases—crystal, silver, or damascene worked in the style of Bidar—have disappeared . . . marble shops that once supplied Italian tiles and statuary to the mansions and baroque gardens of grandees . . . Kalutola's fruit stalls, patronized by the Jewish community, still offer the pick of the orchards . . . A narrow entrance on Lower Chitpur Road leads into Tiretta Bazaar, the colonnaded arcade

where Armenians and Portuguese shopped for birds and beasts. This was the market for selective shoppers; it stocked the choicest foodstuffs, cigars and shoes. Edward Tiretta, a Venetian exile, who became Calcutta's Superintendent of Streets and Bazaars built this market.[24]

Farha often shopped at Tiretta Bazaar, which was close to her home.[25] These congested, bustling cosmopolitan streets contrasted sharply with the ambience and order of imperial or White town, distinguished by its neat, wide streets, and large open maidan.

For Baghdadi Jews the synagogue was a dominant social and community force in the nineteenth century. Members of the community gravitated to the synagogue and its religious ceremonies.[26] In the absence of a centre for meeting, the house of worship was the place for social interaction and exchange, public meetings, the announcement of domestic occurrences, even the place where personal animosities were played out.

Jewish ritual events and festivals were eagerly anticipated social and ceremonial occasions, and Farha enjoyed them immensely, both in Calcutta and with Jewish families overseas. She was an outgoing, gregarious woman who loved people, and was very broad-minded for her day and age. Some of the most elaborate ritual events were connected with marriages and births. There was the engagement ceremony, or 'baat pakka' (meaning 'finalizing the matter' in Hindustani), and the *mileek* (Arabic for engagement celebration). The *mileek* is held at the home of the girl's parents. The groom's family arrives with an array of trays containing flowers and candy. A woman—the *dhakaka*—is the mistress of ceremonies. She is adept at percussion and plays the tambourine while balancing a glass of liquid or the candy tray on her head as she dances to her music. The ring is placed on the bride's finger by her future mother- or father-in-law. Another elaborate ritual was the *khatba* (Arabic for pre-wedding ceremony). This function takes place from a week to three days before the wedding. The climax of this occasion is the applying of henna to the couple's outstretched fingers. The *toowafah* takes place on the Saturday night before the wedding. On this auspicious night the groom once again sends trays of candy, flowers and molasses to the bride, followed by a get-together of both families. The couple steps over a goat or sheep as atonement. After all these ceremonies, which build and strengthen family ties, there is the wedding itself and the sheva brachot (literally 'seven blessings' in Hebrew). These are dinners served in the post-nuptial week, when the wedding ceremony's seven benedictions and sacred songs are chanted. The occasion often lasts well into the morning. Brits, bar mitzvahs, and maftirs were also grand religious, social, and community events.

The observance of festivals, rites, laws, and rituals, expresses and maintains community identity and solidarity and enables its members to become conscious of the social and moral force of the community. Similarly, these ceremonies helped mark Jewish community identity and differentiate it from all others.[27]

During these festive occasions the men grouped together, as did the women, to conduct the rituals and to enjoy themselves separately, but there were no formal partitions between their spaces. All took pleasure in singing, dancing, and listening to Arabic and Hindustani music. For such occasions Farha would dress formally in a *gowan*—an elaborate gown called a *qussah* in Arabic. This coat-dress was buttoned down the front and was typically made of a rich fabric. It had a low-cut neckline that accentuated the bosom and long sleeves widening to the cuff, where there was a slit. A long, thin underdress was worn underneath the coat and covered the bosom. The neck and the borders of the long-sleeved underdress were embroidered or were worked Indian-style.[28] Sometimes, instead of the underdress women wore a front panel covered by an *angiya* (bodice) of fine cloth, usually elaborately embroidered and fastened with straps. The bodice, worn beneath the underdress, had short sleeves and was tied at the back with laces. It, too, was decorated with richly coloured embroidery that remained visible through the thin garment covering it.[29] Under both the dress and underdress Farha wore loose, wide-bottomed trousers, gathered at the waist by a drawstring.[30] Her neck was adorned with strands of pearls, chains with gold coins, or silver lockets. Throughout the Ottoman Empire in the eighteenth and nineteenth century, many women dressed in this style.

On Sabbath each week the women visited each other in the late afternoons when it was no longer hot. They chatted as they drank tea and munched on sunflower or dried watermelon seeds. On Sundays and other holidays Jewish families often went on family picnics and outings to favourite spots such as the Alipur zoo, the Sibpur botanical gardens, and the Eden Gardens. Farha, too, enjoyed these outings very much. Many winters were spent in Madhupur (Bihar), a favourite vacation spot for the

Baghdadi Jewish community.[31] The wealthier Jewish families often owned a winter home there.

Throughout her life Farha lived in rented houses, as did most poor and middle-class Jews. Their homes or apartments were usually in two or three-storey brick buildings with flat roofs. The apartments consisted of three to five large airy rooms—a bedroom or two, an all-purpose room, used primarily for dining, a bathroom and an outside kitchen. The kitchen was often located in the open compound close to the house. The rooms had high ceilings and barred windows, with wooden shutters to keep out the intense afternoon heat. There was usually an attached verandah or courtyard, used for drying clothes and food products, for potted plants, and for sitting out in the sun. Farha dried sunflower seeds, tamarind,[32] sour plums, rinds of pumelo and oranges on large metal trays called *khunchas* out on the terrace or verandah.

Farha's youngest son, Isaac, now an old man in London, told my mother about his home on Metcalfe Street in Calcutta. He recalls an apartment with five rooms, with a dining room and a courtyard in the centre where the sukkah (house built on the Feast of the Tabernacles) was erected. The ground floor of the house was rented out to shops. Isaac admired his mother greatly as an enterprising and shrewd businesswoman. After Saleh died she wanted to maintain her lifestyle, which she managed by finding tenants to occupy a part of the house. My mother recalls another place in which Farha lived when my mother was a young girl.

> I remember one house she lived in on Sooterkin Street (near Bentinck Street). It was on the ground floor and it had a large square open courtyard, which she filled with plants of all kinds. I remember her going out each evening to water her plants with great care. She also kept goats and milked them herself. Keeping plants and goats was usually difficult to do in flats in Calcutta, but having this courtyard made it possible.

Farha's rooms were sparsely furnished with the minimum of decoration. The bedroom had a large bed frame made of wood with a cotton mattress and some pillows. A white mosquito net was attached to the frame. Wooden almirahs were used to store clothes and personal possessions. The family room had an easy chair, a few simple wooden chairs with cane seating, a couple of wide cane *morahs* (stools), and a wooden table. The kitchen had a *kapera*—a wooden cupboard with wire mesh doors to keep out the insects. The *kapera* was mounted on metal trivets containing water to prevent ants from getting in. The water in the kitchen and bathroom was filled in big vats by a bhistiwallah who carried water in a large leather bag from home to home. The kitchen had a chulha, a table for food preparation, and a low tap at ground level for washing utensils. By the thirties and forties the flats that Farha rented in the more Anglicized parts of town had access to running water.

Farha's children and grandchildren remember their dadi fondly. My mother's description captures her love and admiration for her grandmother:

> Dadi was a tall, statuesque woman. She carried her head with a certain dignity, which made her stand out from the others. She held her chin up proudly and one could not help but look up to her. She had brown hair, which was held back in a bun, and her eyes were large and brown. She dressed very well and she was conscious of her carriage. Whatever she wore was of fine quality. Later in her life she became obese and was housebound. But even sitting down she had an air of queenliness. She was very much the family matriarch whose opinion counted. Her support and input on family decisions was always considered valuable. All her children, even in their adult years, revered and respected her.

Farha appreciated the importance of an education and took a keen interest in all her children's schooling. However, none of her daughters finished school, and her sons only went through high school and then started to work. This was fairly typical of most Baghdadi Jewish families who thought that their daughters needed only a basic education to be able to run their homes. They thought it best for their sons to finish school and then learn a trade or join the family business. Typically, among middle-class and poorer Jewish families the boys were sent to the Talmud Torah (the Jewish Boys' School) and the girls to the Jewish Girls' School. Farha encouraged all her children to help in her business and to start businesses of their own. She arranged marriages for her three daughters and provided their trousseaus. Ruby, her youngest daughter, was married around 1929, which was after Saleh died. Farha arranged for her to marry a Jew from Cochin who resided in Calcutta and whose family followed Baghdadi customs. He was well-educated, cultured, and had a dark complexion. Whereas the dark skin of the Cochini Jews was looked down upon by the fair Baghdadi Jews of Calcutta, Farha did not let this deter her from mak-

Above left Baghdadi elder in Arab dress; *right* Simcha Zachariah, an elite lady of the Baghdadi community around the turn of the century, in traditional dress. *Below left* Early twentieth century Baghdadi men and women in traditional costume, *gowans* for the women and a frock coat for the gentleman; *right* changing dress norms, c. 1930s: from the Arabic style 'wrapper' worn by the older women, to Western clothes for the younger ones.

ing this match though many family members advised her against it. Most Baghdadi Jews were colour prejudiced and saw their fair complexion as an asset. Despite these objections, Farha thought he was an excellent partner for her daughter and went ahead with the arrangements. In fact, because Farha inherited money from Baghdad when the match was being made, she spent lavishly on Ruby. Ruby still proudly recalls the rich trousseau her mother provided. It included mahogany almirahs and furniture, a silver dressing set, gold jewellery, and other expensive items. Farha had not been in a position to provide as generously for her older daughters.

All of Farha's children married within the Jewish community and lived most of their lives in India. Her daughters did not have to work for a living. Her children, who studied in English-medium schools, were far more Anglicized than she. They spoke English, wore European clothes, and listened to Western music. Her sons selected their own spouses, as did her daughter Mozelle. However, Ruby's children continued to eat Middle Eastern food, which over the years became more spicy and Indian in its flavours.

During his later years Saleh continued to do business and was able to support his family. His business partner in Calcutta was a Jewish man by the name of Mash-al (later Anglicized by his descendants to Marshall). He and Saleh had a small business selling fez caps between Calcutta and Dacca. The caps were available at their small shop on Chitpore Road. Isaac recalls that the business made a loss and the shop closed after a short time. Family lore has it that Saleh was the first man to import rickshaws to Calcutta from China. We do not know exactly when, but it must have been sometime before 1913-14, for this is when rickshaws came into use in Calcutta.[33] Apparently Saleh brought a hand-pulled rickshaw from China and had Chinese carpenters copy the prototype. He owned several rickshaws and ran this business for a few years. His daughter Dinah's husband, Jacob, subsequently tried to run the business but could not make a success of it either. Saleh sold it when the day-to-day management became too onerous.

Farha helped her husband manage his other business activities as he grew older. The two were extremely attached to each other. I particularly like the description of them sitting on low stools on the verandah or courtyard enjoying a double hookah together in the early evenings. A double hookah has one chillum in the middle but two pipes. It was not unusual for women to smoke. Farha enjoyed smoking her hookah and, when her companion died, she continued to smoke a single hookah. Later she also enjoyed smoking cigarettes. When she was a very old woman, my father often took her a packet of cigarettes—a gesture that endeared him to her.

My grandmother Mary knew Saleh when he was already an older man and described him to my mother:

> He was tall and imposing, the type of man you turned around to take another look at. He had light hair and blue eyes, and till he died in his eighties he walked erect. He never needed glasses and his hearing was unimpaired. Saleh was always well groomed and was outgoing, generous, yet strict with his children. He did not spare the rod and was known to often have used the cane on them but was always very kind and proud of his wife Farha on whom he doted.

As her husband grew older and less mobile, Farha gradually started her own businesses to supplement the family income. Some Baghdadi women worked outside their homes in the late nineteenth and early twentieth century. The 1901 Census reports that sixty-nine Jewish women, including a few European Jews, were employed in Calcutta. Women worked as piece-good dealers, tailors, general merchants, shopkeepers, and domestic help.[34] Four women were teachers. There were seven prostitutes and five women who were singers and actors.[35]

On several mornings Farha set out for Burrabazaar, the large central wholesale market of Calcutta. Sinha writes:

> Burrabazar was a vast and interlocking series of business zones having some features distinct from the China-bazaar or the Cossitola business area of the intermediate town, which tended to lean towards the European town. The cosmopolitan centre of the intermediate town which interpenetrated with these bazaars and business areas had a maritime bias, which clearly distinguished it from Burrabazar.[36]

Farha searched the busy bazaar for beautiful fabrics. She went down the long, winding lanes in this dense shopping area accompanied by a coolie who would carry her purchases in a wide-brimmed cane basket. She wore a long tussore silk coat over her wrapper and her hair in a scarf. She went about on foot or in a hired phaeton, a four-wheeled, horse-drawn carriage. It was not customary then for middle-and upper- class women to go out to the bazaars, though her going was not frowned upon by the Jewish community because circumstances demanded it.

Followed by two coolies, Farha called on wealthier Jewish homes to offer silks, lace, voiles, linen, and velvets. They bought the fabrics and gave them to Jewish seamstresses to sew into garments for bridal trousseaus, as it was not considered appropriate to have Indian male durzees or tailors sew their clothes. It was customary for the bride's family to provide their daughters with bed linen and many sets of outfits—from underwear to outer garments. Even the underwear of Jewish women in that period was elaborate. It was made with cotton and lace, picot-edged, and pin-tucked. The ones who could afford it favoured the number eighteen and gifted that many outfits on auspicious occasions. They believed that the number eighteen signified by gematriya (a mystical method of assigning numbers to the letters of the Hebrew alphabet) translated into the word hai meaning 'life' in Hebrew. Thus, multiples of eighteen were used for charity, for wedding gifts, and for brachot. In addition to the clothing and bed linen, the girl's family provided the bride with gold jewellery and the new couple with a bedroom suite. Farha's finer linens and 'mull-mulls' (fine, soft cottons) were bought for baby clothes, underwear, and household linen. Preparing a layette for the expected baby was an occasion for the women of the bride's family to get together—it was customary for this to be a gift from the grandparents. Special silk outfits and bedclothes decorated with zari (gold thread embroidery) were made. While the women did not necessarily sew all the garments, they selected the fabric, often did the embroidery, and saw to the design details as tailors sewed the clothes. The baby clothes and the cradle were often decorated with amulets.[37] My mother recalls the great detail in which her mother arranged for the clothing of my eldest sister, Esther. She remembers that each of the eighteen outfits had to have a different design!

In the late nineteenth and early twentieth century, many middle-class and poor Jewish women worked as seamstresses and in other small businesses that catered to the needs of the wealthier members of the community. Farha was a good businesswoman, but her rudimentary reading and writing skills made her depend on Saleh to do her accounts. Saleh, then in his eighties, trained Ruby, his youngest and still unmarried daughter, to manage Farha's accounts. As times changed and Farha needed to support her family, she branched out into other businesses. Farha marketed her culinary skills. She made special kosher jams, jellies, preserves, and pickles to sell from her home and to supply to a dealer for export. She super-vised this work in her home with the help of local domestic workers, who did the chopping, stirring, and other preparatory work. Farha was often asked by others in the community to cook *mahbooz* (confections) for wed-dings and other ceremonial occasions. She made *cheese samboosas, almond rings, kakas, date-babas, kulichas, baklavas,* and other baked delicacies. On receiving an order, she prepared all the food and called a baker to her home to have him bake them in his oven. The bakers delivered the goods to her home from where they were picked up by her clientele.

Farha was famed for speciality dishes like *pacha* (a delicacy made from beef intestines) that only a few women knew how to prepare. Her apple *murubba* (where the entire apple, complete with its stalk, was crystallized and set in the jam) was greatly prized. She also prepared rose-and-*kewra* water, called *koom koom*, which was used to offer blessings in the synagogue in memory of the deceased. Mourners took containers of this *koom koom* from person to person to recite the appropriate blessing over spices. Rabbi Musleah elaborates on this custom and explains that *koom koom* was used because its smell was so satisfying it moved the congregation to praise the Almighty.[38] The praise elevated their souls closer to God. It was also used to douse the shrouds that enveloped the dead.

For Passover Farha prepared kosher salt, pepper, spices, and *halek* (Baghdadi *haroset* made from the juice of dates and crushed walnuts), which she sold to a Jewish trader in Calcutta. He in turn exported them across the Far East to the smaller Jewish communities in Rangoon, Singapore, and Penang. This export and import of foods was common in the nineteenth and twentieth centuries. For example, right up till the Second World War, Calcutta Jews primarily cooked in olive oil from Palestine. Dates and many sweetmeats such as *halkoon* (Turkish delight), *baba-khadrasi* (nougat), *halva-rashi* (halva), and *kamrudin* (apricot leather) were imported from Baghdad and later made locally. Farha kept large glass jars of these delights in her almirah and doled them out to her grandchildren when they visited. Throughout the Baghdadi diaspora the same Middle Eastern specialities were relished, as they still are in London, Tel Aviv, and Sydney.

Aside from her business ventures, Farha was well-known in the com-munity for the medicinal herbs that she grew in earthen pots in her small compound or on the verandah. She grew *yas* (myrtle, which she used for the Sabbath benediction), *rehan* (basil for flavouring), and other plants, including aloe vera. Community members sought her advice about natural remedies. She informally counselled women, helped arrange marriages, and offered marriage counselling to community members. She was considered very wise in these matters. Farha was extremely superstitious, as were most Baghdadis, and was apparently able to detect the cause of a sickness or tell who was lying and cheating by reading signs and dreams.

Farha was not a professional marriage broker, but she gave advice on the suitability of partners and the probability of the families getting on well. Marriage brokers were mostly women whose help was sought in 'disposing' of girls who were older or less attractive. When families unfamiliar with each other were introduced, a searching enquiry going back three to four generations was conducted. Matchmaking was quite a competitive business. Fees for this service were standard—the matchmaker received a complete set of clothes for each successful arrangement. When the labours of the broker bore fruit, a tray of candy, flowers, and a piece of jewellery were sent to the girl from the boy's parents.

The more elite Jews moved beyond the narrow confines of the Jewish community and lived in garden homes in the European sections of town. They entertained other members of the elite they knew through business and politics, at their homes or at clubs. These wealthier Baghdadi Jews, who were more Anglicized, looked down on the many members of the community like Farha who did not speak English or dress in a Western style.[39] The elite Jewish families did not mix socially with the less affluent Jews. They sent their children to England or to prestigious missionary schools in Calcutta, while the rest of the community attended the Jewish schools.

The elite mercantile families identified with the British while maintaining good relations with their Indian counterparts. They carried British passports, living 'as though their futures belonged in Europe even though their past was Middle Eastern and their present Asian.'[40] The process of Anglicization among wealthier members of the community was rapid:

> Those members of the elite who remained in India took long vacations in England, adopted the English dress, language and manners and were progressively accepted as marginal members of the European community for many purposes—though in the caste-ridden society of Anglo India it was always clear that they did not quite belong.[41]

Anglicization was less complete further down the social structure, but the community was led and dominated by its elite, mercantile elements.

The Baqaals had a strong Judeo-Arabic cultural identity. A knowledge of Arabic, with limited understanding of Hebrew as the language of the synagogue and ritual practice in the home, enabled Saleh, like most Baghdadi Jewish men, to peruse the Hebrew-Arabic newspapers, which were perhaps the main source of local and overseas news.[42] Farha's children and grandchildren, however, moved away from this identity to adopt what I call an 'Indo-Anglian' identity. I prefer to use this term to distinguish the different ways in which the Baghdadi Jews fused 'Englishness' and 'Indianness' and to distinguish it from the fusion of cultures, and indeed the fusion of two different ethnic groups, created by 'Anglo-Indians.'[43]

In the last decade and a half of her life, Farha witnessed dramatic political upheavals. In 1942, during World War II, the Japanese invaded Burma and were soon at the Indian border. Jews from Singapore, Penang, Kuala Lumpur, and Rangoon escaped the invasion and poured into Calcutta by ship and by land. Most Calcutta Jewish homes made room for these refugees. Farha welcomed family members from Rangoon, whom my mother remembers as the 'Rangoon cousins'. She recalls them as being in their late fifties with grown-up married and unmarried children. Farha helped the Rangoon cousins settle and find jobs in Calcutta. They were entrepreneurs and businessmen who brought a special formula to make bottled drinks. The Rangoon cousins opened a small factory in Calcutta and sold colas and syrups to the American army stationed there. In less than ten years they had made enough money for the family to emigrate to the United States and buy a house in Los Angeles. Many of the Jewish refugees from other diaspora communities married Calcutta Jews. Thus immediately during and after the War the community grew. This expansion, however, was rapidly followed by the shrinking of the community when India gained her independence. After independence, waves of Jews started leaving Calcutta.

Farha, in the later years of her life, like many other members of the Jewish community, moved from the Canning Street area to the area between Bentinck Street and Central Avenue (today known as Chittaranjan Avenue). This movement from the Grey to what were predominantly the White areas of town started in the 1920s and was another mark of the Anglicization taking place among even the middle and lower-middle class

Jews. In the thirties and forties many Jews moved further south to the New Market area around Lindsay, Sudder, and Marquis streets, and Kyd and Hartford lanes, which had become a predominantly Jewish enclave by that time. A small shul was built in Sudder Street so that the Jews now living in this area could attend regular prayer services within walking distance from their homes. Towards the end of her life Farha also moved to this part of town. She rented a room and bath in Tottee Lane, adjoining the home of my grandfather and grandmother, Elias and Mary, so she could be near her family. Older people like her did not leave Calcutta unless they were living with their families who decided to move. My mother describes Farha in her later years:

> She cooked for us, told us stories from the Bible and anecdotes from her childhood. She was a good storyteller and we laughed a lot as we listened to her. She spoke to us in Hindi, Arabic and a few words of English thrown into the mix as well. She was our fun grandmother. She was not someone to sit alone and sew. She made up card games, challenged us in touli (backgammon) and enjoyed smoking her hookah.

Farha was looked after till her death by my maternal grandparents, Elias and Mary. They had a full time ayah (personal maid) take care of her. She stayed in a room attached to their home. Farha was never sick but by this time had become quite obese and was not able to move around much. Relatives and friends visited her regularly, and she still followed the affairs of the community eagerly. She eventually died in Calcutta in her mid eighties in 1958 and is buried in the Calcutta cemetery. At that time she had about 250 direct descendants, some of whom had left Calcutta to pursue their futures in many parts of the world.

Farha's life should not be read as the story of one woman alone. It provides rare glimpses into the material and conceptual worlds of middle-class women from this diaspora community; few primary or secondary documents yield information on their lives.[44] There is a dearth of information on women in the documents on the Baghdadi Jewish diaspora, just as there is relatively little writing about the women of the numerous smaller minority communities that thrived in colonial India. Working against the tide, the experiences of women who were not part of the European or Indian mainstream show us that they were active in both the public and the private domain as householders, travellers, traders, and businesswomen.

Farha's narrative discloses the processes by which a generation of middle-class Jews shifted from one dual or hyphenated identity, Judeo-Arabic, to another, Judeo-British. In this process of 'transculturation',[45] their Jewish identity remained the constant and primary identity—the first part of their hyphenated selves. Farha's story highlights the 'deterritorialized' nature of the community, in which identity was delinked from territory. Its members moved fluidly across borders and large geographic spaces but were able to maintain strong boundaries and real communities even as they moved. The shift from Baghdad to other locations in the diaspora, and subsequent moves to yet other destinations, were not traumatic. Rather, these diasporic movements are better understood as a historic process through which community members flourished. This diaspora was quintessentially a 'diaspora of hope'.

The Baghdadi Jews were in many ways an imagined community, a 'community of sentiment' tied together by Jewish beliefs and religious custom. Baghdadi Jews identified strongly with each other, and saw themselves as a 'community' whether they lived in Calcutta or Shanghai. They believed in and acted on their common identity. They were interconnected in numerous on-going ways. There were several means, such as visits, their sharing of rituals and customs, that made this identification with other Baghdadi Jews still stronger.[46]

The social, religious, and traditional connections among Jews across this diaspora enabled a strong sense of community identity to emerge despite the great economic differences between them. They felt a sense of deep, horizontal comradeship, regardless of the actual inequality and exploitation that prevailed among them. While there were certainly great class differences there was a pervasive acceptance of each other as Jews and a commitment to help each other in times of need. This commitment to one another was manifested through the establishment of several charitable trusts. Funded by the Sassoons and Ezras, Gubbays and Meyers, these trusts were established to take care of impoverished Jews from birth to burial. For example, poorer Jewish students were supported by community money and attended the Jeshuruan Free School, the Elias Meyer Free School and the Talmud Torah. Women's travel further knitted this community together. Their visits back and forth played a considerable role in making Jews across the diaspora feel part of a community despite the geographical distances that separated them.

Notes

Flyleaf: Farha in her old age.

1 Stanley Jackson, in *The Sassoons* (New York: E. P. Dutton & Co., 1968), discusses the ways in which the Sassoons entertained the British aristocracy and political figures in England, India and the Far East. He notes that in the last two decades of the century the Court Circular was rarely without some daily reference to the Sassoons. Whereas the prestigious Baghdadi families from Calcutta may not have entertained as lavishly and were not as notable, they too interacted with the economically and politically powerful British in Calcutta and abroad and adapted to British ways. Leading members of the Calcutta community were invited to the Viceroy's levees and celebrations and helped to organize some of the latter. For more information on this topic see Joan G. Roland, *Jews in British India: Identity in a Colonial Era* (Hanover, NH: University Press of New England, 1989), pp. 56–64.

2 It was not until 1911 that Delhi was made the capital of the British Empire of India.

3 Sinha in Chaudhuri (ed.), *Calcutta the Living City*, p. 33.

4 Albert Memmi in *The Colonizer and the Colonized* (Boston: Beacon Press, 1967), comments on the dialogue between colonizer and the colonized and the influence they had on each other's institutions and forms, and notes the hybridity of architectural forms and styles of colonial cities. 'The buildings are patterned after the colonizer's favorite designs; the same is true of the street names, which recall the faraway provinces from which he came. Occasionally, the colonizer starts a neo-Eastern style, just as the colonized imitates European style' (p. 104). Calcutta's buildings reflected this accommodation between the colonial rulers and the local elite.

5 Pradip Sinha, *Calcutta in Urban History* (Calcutta: Firma K. L. M., 1978), p. 30.

6 This information on the community economic structure was obtained from Rabbi Ezekiel Musleah. In personal discussion with me he contradicted the breakdown of the community described by Timberg (in Katz (ed.), *Studies in Indian Jewish Identity*), where it is stated that the 'Baghdadi community was middle-class tending towards the prosperous in composition, with a considerable number of very wealthy and few

poor members' (p. 141). Musleah argues that Timberg was not witness to the miserable conditions, destitution and penury in the heart of the Jewish community.

7 Jacob Sapir, the envoy from Jerusalem in 1860, noted: 'The Baghdadians marry only virgin girls below the age of seventeen years. Beauty and talent are sought after. So the more particular bring out their wives from Baghdad, Syria and the Holy Land. They do not marry for money.' See Musleah, *On the Banks of the Ganga*, p. 201. Arranged marriages were the order of the day till well into the twentieth century.

8 The prayerbook was in the possession of his grandson in Australia but is now with Flower Silliman. Rabbi Musleah translated the writing, which included the dates and places of the birth of his children.

9 Despite the information, which I received earlier from her sister Ruby, that Dinah was born in Baghdad, I now believe that Saleh's precise and meticulously recorded information is accurate.

10 Ruth Fredman Cernea 'Promised Land and Domestic Arguments: The Conditions of Jewish Identity in Burma,' in Katz (ed.), *Studies of Indian Jewish Identity*, p.164.

11 A maftir is the occasion when a boy reads a portion of the torah for the first time at a Sabbath service and makes a donation to the synagogue. As the boy becomes a man, he reads the prayers on auspicious occasions and continues to make donations.

12 The Nahoums still own a bakery and a popular confectionery store in the New Market.

13 This information was provided by Rabbi Ezekiel Musleah. He has most of the Jewish birth and marriage records of the Calcutta Jews in his keeping.

14 My mother was told that one of Tufahah's daughters was a secretary to David Ben Gurion.

15 Katz made this point when he described the Baghdadi community as living in India but not being of India. He contrasts them with the Cochin and Bene Israel Jews who were much more assimilated. Of course these other groups of Jews had been in India much longer, whereas the Baghdadi Jews came to India with the British. However, though the Baghdadis were loyal to their British overlords they did not identify with them. Socially they isolated themselves from both British and Indian society because of their religious taboos and a deep fear of assimilation. See

Katz (ed.), *Studies of Indian Jewish Identity*.

16 This maintenance of boundaries between Jews and other communities was not unusual in the Indian context, where the dominant tradition emphasizes separate social spheres among different religions and castes. Despite this 'boundary maintenance' theirs was a 'harmonic co-existence'. Timberg notes that the 'foreignness' of the Baghdadi was not a disturbing element in traditional Indian society, with its easy tolerance, but compartmentalization of differences. This 'harmonic co-existence' was maintained despite the British obsession with classifying the Indian population, or their 'divide and rule policy.' See Timberg, 'Indigenous and Non-Indigenous Jews', p. 150.

17 Musleah, *On the Banks of the Ganga*, p. 67.

18 My mother visited the shul and noted a plaque at the entrance that commemorates the endowment her family made to the synagogue.

19 Musleah, *On the Banks of the Ganga*, p. 68.

20 Musleah notes that the precious unpublished manuscripts of Hacham Shlomo are lost forever in the Calcutta Genizah. Unlike the Cairo Genizah, the Calcutta Genizah comprises a well of water for the disintegration of religious writings and articles. See *On the Banks of the Ganga*, p. 93.

21 All this information about Hacham Twena is from Musleah, *On the Banks of the Ganga*. Ruby's daughter, my aunt Seemah who now lives in Israel, married into the Twena family.

22 I am using the term Sephardic in the way it is used today in reference to non-European Jews. However, I am aware that Sephardic Jews originally referred specifically to those Jews expelled from Spain and Portugal since 1492 who flourished as an exile community in many parts of the world including in the Ottoman Empire. The Sephardim kept their Spanish culture and maintained cultural links with Spain. The Baghdadi Jews of India often referred to themselves as Sephardim in reference to their liturgical traditions rather than to their geographic origins.

23 Musleah, *On the Banks of the Ganga*, p. 184.

24 Chaudhuri, *Calcutta the Living City*, vol. 1, p. 30.

25 Over the course of the twentieth century Tiretta Bazaar came to be dominated by Chinese merchants. As this community has also dwindled over the last twenty years due to emigration to the West, the cosmopolitan character of the bazaar is almost gone. However, at the dawn of

the twenty-first century it is still the only place in Calcutta where one can get dimsum for breakfast and other Chinese specialities.

26 The size and grandeur of the synagogues they built testify to the centrality of the synagogue in community life. The synagogues housed many elaborate torah scrolls. The scrolls, cases and finials were originally brought from Iraq but later local artists were commissioned to make the cases. The polygonal or cylindrical cases with onion domes were overlaid with hammered silver sheets or covered with velvet fabric and decorated with floral patterns. To read about and see pictures of the torah scrolls consult Orpa Slapak (ed.), *The Jews of India: A Story of Three Communities* (Jerusalem: The Israel Museum, 1995), pp. 71–6.

27 Margaret Abraham, 'Marginality and Disintegration of Community Identity among the Jews of India,' in Katz (ed.), *Studies in Indian Jewish Identity,* p. 190.

28 Slapak (ed.), *The Jews of India*, p. 139.

29 Slapak contends that this *angiyah* was adopted from local customs. Slapak (ed.), *The Jews of India*.

30 Slapak also says that women who wore the *qussah* to the synagogue would cover themselves from head to toe with a white fabric (*chadder*). Slapak (ed.), *The Jews of India*.

31 Madhupur, which is not very far from Calcutta, offers a salubrious climate in the winter. In the last decade of the nineteenth century, Calcutta Jews, rich and poor, wintered there. For a month or two it was a festive, lively place. At one time, daily and Sabbath services were held there and a sefer torah was transported there. See Musleah, *On the Banks of the Ganga*, p. 56.

32 The word tamarind comes from Tamar Hindi which, in Hebrew, means dates from India (Hind).

33 See Nisith Ranjan Ray, *Calcutta The Profile of a City* (Calcutta: K. P Bagchi & Company, 1986). In addition he notes that bicycles made their first appearance on the streets of Calcutta in 1889, motor cars in 1896 and taxis in 1906. The first horse drawn buses plied in 1830.

34 Whereas the Census lists Jewish women as servants I think they would be treated more like help. These women would most surely have worked for very wealthy Jewish families and played supervisory roles in such homes, where most of the other servants would be non-Jews. By virtue of their being Jewish they would have been treated differently from the

other servants.

35 This information is taken from Esmond Ezra, who is quoted by Timberg in Katz (ed.), *Studies of Indian Jewish Identity*, p. 139. The Calcutta Census for 1901 showed that there were five-hundred and eleven males and sixty nine females employed in ninety eight different professions.

36 Sinha, *Calcutta in Urban History*, p. 58.

37 The amulets were made from gall-nuts and sometimes decorated with gold tinsel, or blue glazed beads, cowries shells or cloves of garlic. Silver pendants were engraved with amuletic formulas. These and other details regarding the Baghdadi ceremonies and traditions for the new-born, including pictures of some material objects, are in Slapak (ed.), *The Jews of India*, pp. 159–61.

38 Musleah, *On the Banks of the Ganga.*

39 Roland, *Jews in British India*, p.120.

40 Cernea in Katz (ed.), *Studies of Indian Jewish Identity*, p. 163.

41 Timberg in Katz (ed.), *Studies of Indian Jewish Identity*, p. 141.

42 The three leading Judeo-Arabic newspapers were the *Paerah, Mebasser* and *Maggid Mesharim.*

43 Whereas many Britishers living in India were referred to as Anglo-Indians because of their long association with India, I am referring to Anglo-Indians as those of mixed race, a group that formed quite a large community in India. The Anglo-Indian community was given distinct privileges under the British: certain professions and jobs were set aside for them. The community had its own distinct culture and social insti-tutions. When the British left India, Anglo-Indians lost their favoured status and privileges. Many Anglo-Indians emigrated to England, Australia, Canada and the United States but many also decided to iden-tify with India and stayed on.

44 Two memoirs and a novel have some accounts of the ways in which the upper-middle and upper-class Baghdadi Jews lived. See Flower Elias, *The Jews of Calcutta: The Autobiography of a Community, 1798-1972* (Calcutta: The Jewish Association of Calcutta, 1974); Esmond Ezra, *Turning Back the Pages: A Chronicle of Calcutta Jewry* (3 vols. London: Brookside Press, 1986), and Virginia Courter, *Flowers in the Blood* (New York: Dutton, 1990). Sally Solomon of the Calcutta Jewish community has written *Hooghly Tales* (London: David Ashley Publishing House, 1998), in which she reminisces about what it meant to grow up Jewish

in Calcutta. This account is from a middle-class perspective and since she is just a few years older than my mother I have drawn on her memories and insights for the chapter on Flower. Esther David of the Bene Israel community from Ahmedabad has written a novel, *The Walled City* (Madras: Manas, 1997). She traces the lives of three generations of Jewish women in an extended family and describes their struggle to maintain a Jewish identity in a predominantly Hindu environment. There is also an account of a woman from the Cochin community.

45 Mary Louise Pratt says that ethnographers use the term transculturation to describe how subordinated or marginal groups 'select and invent from materials transmitted to them by a dominant or metropolitan culture.' While they cannot control what is transmitted to them, they are more able to determine which aspects of the culture they will absorb into their own and how to employ what they have transferred. See Pratt, *Imperial Eyes*, p. 6.

46 Cernea, in Katz (ed.), *Studies of Indian Jewish Identity*, discusses the many ways in which Jewish community identity was forged.

Mary:
Coming Home to the Mount of Olives

*M*ARY'S PERSONALITY AND LIFE CONTRAST SHARPLY with that of her indomitable mother-in-law, Farha. Whereas Farha was expansive, gregarious, and high-spirited, Mary was inward-looking, serious, and rigid in her lifestyle and views. Farha was tall and handsome, while my grandmother was five feet tall and shrank further over the years. Farha was popular and the life of a party, whereas my grandmother did not like to draw attention to herself and was very much a loner. Farha was lavish and carefree in her outlook on life, timid Mary followed rules scrupulously. My mother's recollection of her brother Eric's bar mitzvah illustrates the contrast:

When Eric was celebrating his bar mitzvah, preparations were being made for the fish lunch that customarily followed the tefilim-wearing ceremony. Mummy [Mary] was worrying about the preparations that had to be made as well as how they could afford such a meal for the extended family. Dadi [Farha], on the other hand, who was dependent on my parents for her income, had no such worries. She lived for the day and always thought big. She encouraged my father to go to the wholesale market and buy the biggest possible fish for this important family event. My father came home with a fish that was larger than Eric, and Dadi was delighted with this catch. She summoned my aunts and the other women relatives and together they set about cleaning, preparing and cooking an elaborate multi-course fish meal. The meal included *seluna* (a fish stew with rice), fried fish with fried eggplant, and fish *chitanee*—a vinegar-based curry. Mummy was very thankful to be left out of the cooking and happily let Dadi run the show. Dadi was in her element—cooking and seeing us all enjoy the fruits of her work. We still remember this wonderful feast; we talked about it for many years after.

Farha was worldly-wise, whereas Mary was bookish and learned in Jewish law and mysticism. Farha came from a mercantile family, Mary from a devout religious lineage. With such different temperaments and outlooks it is not surprising that there were tensions between them. Mary was certainly not Farha's choice of daughter-in-law. Though her other four sons also chose their own brides, Farha more readily approved of their choices because the other women were more flamboyant and lively than Mary. Yet it was her eldest son, Elias, and his plain wife, Mary—the least well-to-do of all her children—who supported Farha throughout her long life and tended scrupulously to her needs. Towards the later part of Farha's life she came to appreciate Mary more, for she was her pillar of support. Despite their differences they became very fond of each other.

Mary's religious lineage dates far back in Jewish history. Her mother, Simcha Abraham, was born in approximately 1874 in El Ozeir, on the banks of the river Tigris in Baghdad. El Ozeir is an important pilgrimage site and one that was particularly close to the hearts of Calcutta Jews because it was there that Ezra the Prophet was buried two thousand years ago. It has remained a sacred site for Jews and Muslims throughout the region. A traveller in the mid-nineteenth century describes the tomb:

> Three days' journey down the Tigris in the middle of the desolate and barren desert El Ozeir, rises, on the shore of the river, a large square building, in which is the tomb of Ezra . . . Although in the midst of the desert, and surrounded by tribes of Arab robbers, there is nothing to fear for the safety of these treasures; as, from the veneration which the Arabs pay to the tomb of Ezra, they are safe from being robbed, and, according to tradition, no robber would be able to leave that sanctuary without having first restored to its place that which he had taken away.
>
> The ships cast anchor not far from his tomb and all travellers, without distinction of faith, betake themselves to it, in order to pray. The stranger who has spent some days in the desert cannot divest himself of a deep religious impression when, in the middle of the wilderness, he perceives this wonderful tomb.[1]

Simcha's forebears were caretakers of the tomb for as long as records exist. Over the generations her family was entrusted to carry out this holy duty. As part of their religious obligations they trained their sons to be teachers, rabbis, mohels, sofers and hazans. These religiously trained men either served in these various capacities in El Ozeir or were sent to serve other Baghdadi Jewish communities throughout the Middle East.

Since medieval times this dispersed Jewish network of communities was linked by kinship ties, business, travel, and loyalty to defined religious centres like Baghdad, Jerusalem, and El Ozeir. As the reach of Jewish communities spread to still more distant areas, these religious men went further afield to sustain the ritual and religious aspects of Jewish community life. Extending this tradition and following the creation of new empires (this time European ones), Simcha's elder brothers were sent in the late nineteenth century to Shanghai, where their religious knowledge was required by a young but prosperous Middle Eastern Jewish community. It was through sending their sons to conduct such jobs that religious families were able to provide for their children through the generations.

In the 1890s Simcha and her youngest brother, Abraham Abraham, then in their teens, were waiting for their family to save enough money to purchase them passages to Shanghai, where their older brothers lived. In the mean time a cholera epidemic claimed the lives of their parents and forced Abraham to find work immediately. Through family connections he found a job in the home of the wealthy Sassoon family of Bombay (also known as the 'Rothschilds of the East'). Mrs Flora (Farha) Hayeem Sassoon,[2] the second wife of Sir David Sassoon, required the services of a mashgiyach (supervisor of kosher kitchens) to make sure that dietary laws were observed in their opulent home in the Poona hills. Abraham was entrusted to ensure that the non-Jewish servants in the kitchen kept strict kashrut. Only the wealthiest in the community could afford such help.[3] After working for a few years in the Sassoon household Abraham found a way for Simcha to join him.

When Mrs Sassoon was ailing and required the services of a nurse–companion, Abraham recommended his sister for the job. Simcha left El Ozeir and travelled by boat to Bombay to take care of the elderly Mrs Sassoon and to be with her brother. She looked after her for a year or two before the lady died. (Simcha told my mother that Mrs Sassoon died in her arms.) In appreciation for her devotion Mrs Sassoon bequeathed Simcha a sum of approximately Rs 2000. Apparently this sum enabled Abraham and Simcha to travel to Calcutta, then a prosperous Baghdadi

Jewish enclave, to find a suitable marriage partner for Simcha. Because she had no parents, it was Abraham's duty to arrange her marriage. The money from Mrs Sassoon also provided a modest dowry, which was customary among the Baghdadi Jews. Simcha married Ezra Shooker sometime after 1896. Ezra, a religious man who had come to Calcutta from Baghdad, was fifteen years older than Simcha and had limited economic prospects. Abraham, having done his duty by Simcha, followed his initial plan and travelled eastwards to Shanghai to join his elder brothers. His family lived there till the end of World War II. Simcha visited her family in Shanghai at least thrice in her lifetime, travelling as a deck passenger—the only way she could afford to travel.

Simcha and her husband were very observant. Ezra went twice a day to pray at the synagogue. (This was in keeping with the Sephardic practice where the afternoon Mincha and Maariv are combined in one service). It was partially for this reason that Jews like him, who were Sabbath-observant and regular synagogue attendees, could not hold regular employment.[4] Ezra bought and sold petty items of food and clothing from his home in Chattawalla Lane in the part of Calcutta where poor and middle-class Jews resided. Because Ezra did not earn enough money to make ends meet and was also quite miserly, Simcha worked to provide enough food for her children. She saved up money to purchase an old Singer sewing machine and did sewing and mending for the middle-class members of the community. My mother recalls Simcha at work in her aunt's home:

> Granny had a tall, lean body, deeply wrinkled olive skin, and a prominent nose and chin. She sat clothed in a long cotton wrapper with her grey hair tied back severely in a knot and covered partially with a kerchief. With her sewing machine on a low wooden stool, she sat on the floor with her knees hunched up near her chest while she turned the wheel of the Singer machine as she sewed and mended for extra money. She took short breaks on the balcony where she puffed on a cigarette or *bidi* (cheap indigenous smoke) as she watched us play.

The Shooker family earnings were so meagre that they had to rely heavily on Jewish charities to educate and provide for their five children.[5] The charities provided them with money during the festivals, clothing, and other necessities. The school, too, helped the poorer students with tuition fees, clothing, books, and lunches. With the help of these various charities they, and others like them, were able to eke out an existence. Despite the assistance, Mary, Simcha's middle daughter, recalled going to bed hungry on many a night, having eaten only bread and tea.

Mary was born in Calcutta in 1901 and grew up in this materially and socially poor, but devout, Jewish environment. She had three brothers and a sister, Mathana (Matty), to whom she remained very close all her life. The Shookers lived in two large rooms in Chattawalla Lane with Jewish, Chinese, Anglo-Indian, and Armenian neighbours. They spoke Arabic at home and Hindustani to the servants and in the street. Simcha did understand English but almost never spoke it. At school the children mastered the English language and were exposed to Western ideas and ways. Mary was a scholarship student at the Jewish Girls' School from 1904 through 1916. By the time she attended the school, it was fairly well-established.

The Jewish Girls' School was opened in 1881 by members of the Jewish community. Education for Jewish girls paralleled the development of girls' education in Calcutta.[6] Before its opening Jewish girls had attended other schools. The poorest in the community attended the Old Mission School, a Christian school that was interested in proselytizing.[7] In part the Jewish Girls' School was opened so that Jewish girls would not fall prey to Christian influences.[8] The school was run on decidedly British lines, although at the core of the school's mission was a commitment to providing students with a Jewish education. Alongside a British-style curriculum the students were instructed in Hebrew prayerbook and the Old Testament. The narrative parts of the Bible were taught in English translation in 'Scripture' classes, while the Hebrew text was never learned with any real level of understanding. To help students read Hebrew fluently, if mechanically, became the limited goal of local Jewish educators. Whereas religious subjects were always taught by Jewish teachers, almost all the other teachers in the early twentieth century were Anglo-Indians.

The school was committed to providing a sound British-oriented education because everything English was associated with opportunities for advancement. Victorian ideals for middle-class women guided the educational curriculum and shaped the school environment. Women were socialized to be docile, gentle, chaste, and nurturing. The students were trained to be good mothers who could provide their children with proper education and values. They learned needlework, read the scriptures, and were exposed to suitable works of English literature. In a discussion of colonial strategies for the 'education of the natives' Gauri Viswanathan considers why Indians strove to acquire the moral and intellectual refinements of the British. She argues that the English literary text 'functioned as a surrogate Englishman in his highest and most perfect state' and quotes from Trevelyan's essay 'On the Education of the People of India' (1838): '[The Indians] daily converse with the best and wisest Englishmen through the medium of their works, and from ideas, perhaps higher ideas of our nation than if their intercourse with it were of a more personal kind.'[9] Through this exposure to English literature students like my grandmother did develop a high regard for British culture, and emulated British values.[10] The students at the Jewish Girls' School also studied Latin and French.

Mary's exposure to Western ideas ran parallel to a strict adherence to Jewish law and to Baghdadi customs and traditions at home, in the community, and in school. In the early twentieth century, when she was a student there, the Jewish Girls' School still had a decidedly informal and Baghdadi character. The students did not wear uniforms—the wealthier girls wore expensive dresses and the poorer students like Mary wore plainer skirts and blouses to school. Teachers taught from comfortable armchairs and the school was characterized as having a relaxed and somewhat easygoing atmosphere.[11] In 1929, Miss Ramah Luddy, a Calcutta Jewish woman trained in England, became the school principal. She enforced greater discipline: the comfortable armchairs were replaced by armless chairs, uniforms were introduced, and formal physical education and gym requirements were made mandatory. These changes were considered more modern and Western. Miss Luddy was greatly admired for her ability to run the school on more professional lines and remains a legend in the community.[12]

While the poor and middle-class girls attended the Jewish Girls' School, the wealthy attended schools like the Calcutta Girls' School, Welland Goldsmith, and, later, Loreto House. These schools catered to the more cosmopolitan and privileged members of Calcutta society. They enrolled Anglo-Indians, Parsis, Jews, and elite Indian students. Some girls from the Jewish elite had private tutors at home. The elite Jews mixed more freely with Europeans and upper-class Indians as well as with the elite from other minority communities. They travelled outside Calcutta and abroad.[13] Mary's world and theirs did not intersect.

According to her school reports, Mary proved to be a diligent and dedicated student.[14] She was among the first generation of girls in the com-

Mary and Elias Abraham at their wedding, with nephew Josh, 1921.

munity to finish her high school degree, in 1916. Her family and friends respected her for her 'book' knowledge and sought her guidance and advice on many matters. For Mary, the Jewish Girls' School was her compass and her anchor at once, giving her intellectual opportunities and a sense of her place in the world. She desired to continue her education and aspired to become a teacher. A few of her contemporaries had similar aspirations and were the first to dedicate themselves to establishing professional careers. Among others, Ramah Musleah, a few years junior to Mary, decided not to marry and dedicated her life to teaching, a profession she cherished all her life; Tabby Solomon became a dentist; and Sarah Abraham became a math teacher at the Jewish Girls' School after training at a teachers' seminary in Dow Hill, Kurseong (West Bengal), and subsequently continued teaching when she emigrated to London.

Mary wished to train as a teacher too and sought to attend Dow Hill. Simcha did not allow her to go there, even though her daughter received a scholarship. Since it was a Christian school, Mary would have had to break Sabbath and eat non-kosher food, practices which were unacceptable to her parents. Instead, Mary trained at the Jewish Girls' School in the kindergarten under the supervision of a trained teacher. On completion of this apprenticeship she was appointed as a teacher by the school and taught there for several years in the kindergarten and later in the second grade. After that she ventured into private tutoring and worked in the homes of wealthy Jews, including the Zachariahs and the Arakies.

Mary was among the first generation of Calcutta Jews not to have an arranged marriage. She met her husband, Elias Abraham (Farha's eldest son), in the synagogue and in the neighbourhood. On a few occasions they went to the movies and met at Jewish community functions. They were not chaperoned during their times together, but they strictly adhered to Victorian notions of proper courtship patterns. Although Elias's mother did not quite approve of the match, the young couple went ahead with their marriage plans. Mary saved to pay for her own modest dowry, which consisted of bedroom furniture, a few dresses, and some linens. In 1921 when they married, Mary was twenty years old, and Elias twenty-three. Their simple wedding ceremony took place in the Neveh Shalome synagogue and was followed by a small reception in the Jewish Girls' School hall. At the reception, family and friends enjoyed Iraqi Jewish sweetmeats and savoury preparations.

Less affluent Jews often held their wedding receptions in the synagogue, while the wealthy held theirs in garden homes and big hotels.
Mary's was decidedly a modern, Western-style wedding—quite different
from the Baghdadi extravaganzas of the previous generation. Mary wore a
calf-length white dress with a veil and train and carried a small bouquet of
flowers. Two flower girls and a pageboy made up her wedding party.

The wealthy women of the Jewish community led quite glamorous
social lives. They mingled in Calcutta's cosmopolitan society, playing
bridge, mahjong, rummy, and other card games, as well as attending garden parties and balls. They took lessons in painting, Western music, and
needlework at home. Mary's life, however, was narrowly circumscribed:
her world was the school, her family, and the synagogue. Jewish festivals
were her social highlights. Mary loved to read English romance novels and
my mother tells me that among her favourite authors were Marie Correlli
and H. Ryder Haggard. Even greater than her love for reading was her passion for the movies, which does seem odd given her puritanical nature.
Mary could not afford to go to the movies before she started earning a living. Once she did, she went regularly to the cinema because movies were
an inexpensive form of entertainment that afforded her great pleasure.[15]
Most of the movies that Mary saw as a young woman and throughout her
middle years were American movies, which dominated the Indian market.[16]

While Hollywood was a major presence in India in the early twentieth century, an indigenous film industry had already taken root in India,
with Bombay and Calcutta as its chief centres. Greatly impacted by colonial influences, these booming port cities had a commercially successful
class that could adopt Western visual technologies and exploit these technologies for profit. According to film historian Sumita Chakravarty, 'Just
as Indian photographers and studios proliferated soon after the introduction
of the camera to India in the 1840s, so the arrival of the motion picture
attracted a large number of business people, artists and craftspeople into
film production and exhibition.'[17] Few members of Calcutta's Jewish community, however, were interested in Indian cinema, despite the booming
film industry.[18] In this early period there were several Baghdadi Jewish
actresses from Bombay who became major stars in Indian films—Ruby
Meyer, with the screen-name Sulochana, and Florence Ezekiel, otherwise
known as the glamorous star Nadira. From my conversations with many
women in the community it seems that these film stars, Indianized for the
screen, were considered beyond the pale of the Jewish community. They

were included in the community as long as they kept their film world distinctly apart. Some Iraqi Jews did, however, enjoy the Indian dancing and songs that were a major feature of the films. As for Mary, she never saw an Indian film in her life and never listened to Indian film songs.

During this period most Indian audiences saw many more American films than those made in India or in other countries. Mary loved the romantic silent movies that were popular through the twenties. My mother says that Mary's favourite stars were Rudolph Valentino and Theda Bara. Mary, always sentimental and a dreamer, particularly enjoyed American romantic movies and it is likely that some of her ideas about romance came from Hollywood. The films projected new cultural forms that young people were eager to imitate.[19] I wonder whether dream-makers knew that their films were being watched avidly by female viewers like Mary in the British colonies. Mary drew on images created in the United States to establish her own ideas and representations of the modern woman she sought to be and it may well be that the film representations of women's roles enabled her to choose her own partner and contemplate a career.

Mary was not the only member of her family mesmerized by the movies and movie stars. The lure of the movies was so palpable that her younger brother, Isaac, wrote short film scripts that he sent to Universal Studios, hoping that they would be picked up. He dreamed of becoming part of that glamorous and far-away world. He eventually ran away in his early twenties to see if he could make it in the movie business. He first went to New York and worked as a bellboy there to pay his way onward to Hollywood. He tried to enter the movie industry but met with no success. He returned home to Calcutta quite crestfallen and never really settled down.[20]

Through the newsreels at the films and through the British press in India, Mary followed the lives of the British royal family with avid interest—this was another form of romance, consumption, and spectacle. She and her sister, Matty, discussed the lives of the royal family in great detail and loved the pomp and pageantry associated with them. They read about the royal family, collected their pictures, and eagerly watched their lives unfold in the documentary newsreels screened before the feature film. This fascination with the British royal family continued into their old age and was an expression of their identification with Britain and the Empire.

Mary's husband, Elias, held a steady job. He was among the first generation of Jews to work in British firms and government service. Elias worked for the British Port Commissioners of Calcutta as a licensed measurer. His job entailed the measuring of jutes and gunnies, two chief export crops of Bengal, before export. Special measurements were used to value these commodities. Working as a civil servant required him to work on the Sabbath. For this reason Jews had previously shunned such jobs, preferring to work in their own businesses and, after the first World War, for rapidly expanding Jewish companies. Breaking with tradition, Elias was the only Jew in his field of work.

While Europeans were his superiors, he worked alongside Anglo-Indians, who were given preferential treatment in obtaining government jobs. Indians at that time were not employed in these professions, allowing Anglo-Indian men to dominate jobs in the railways, police force, and post office that were explicitly set aside for them. Since Jewish and Armenian men also spoke English and had adopted many Western ways, they were accepted in these services. As the eldest son, Elias became the provider for his widowed mother, Farha, and his younger siblings. While Elias was able to bring in a steady income, his earnings did not suffice for him to fully support his immediate family as well. Thus, Mary continued working at the Jewish Girls' School. After she had children she found it more convenient to work as a private tutor in wealthier Jewish homes, where she could determine her own schedule and working hours. Like her mother, Simcha, Mary's earnings were important for the maintenance of her family.

The apartment Elias and Mary rented on Weston Street was modestly furnished, but European in style. The furnishings included beds, almirahs, sofas, armchairs, sideboards, showcases, and a large dining table. The windows were always covered with pretty chintz curtains. Wealthy Jews were able to buy their furniture from prestigious companies like Lazarus of Calcutta, a European firm that employed Indian carpenters to make English-style mahogany and teak furniture. Mary's furniture was made by local carpenters who copied the styles of the more expensive furniture companies. There were few pictures on the walls and no Indian decorations in Jewish homes. Large colour posters with the faces of Rudolph Valentino, Ramon Navarro, and Edward, the Prince of Wales, were among the few pictures in Mary's otherwise starkly decorated home—they had pride of place in her bedroom. Flower remembers her father teasing Mary about her passion for the movies, saying: 'She has pictures of only famous

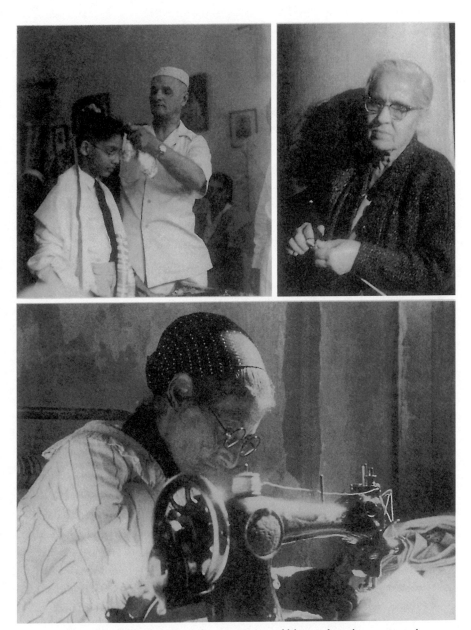

Above left Elias at his nephew's bar mitzvah; *right* Mary would knit and crochet continuously, even while visiting her grandchildren. *Below* Simcha Shooker, wearing the traditional head scarf or *yasmah*.

men in her room, so I do not fit in there.' Carved Chinese camphor-wood chests and satsuma vases and tea sets were prized and popular in many middle-class homes. Mary, too, owned a chest and a satsuma china tea set.

Mary, like most other Baghdadi Jews, owned a few ritual and ceremonial items that graced her home. These items—a Sabbath lamp called a *tirya*, a *hanukkiya,* and a matzah basket—remained as constant reminders of her Baghdadi heritage. The *hanukkiya* was triangular in form with one glass lamp at the apex of the triangle and eight lamps in a line at its base.[21] The *tirya*, like the *hanukkiya*, was made of beaten brass. With a central glass lamp and six surrounding lamps, the *tirya* was shaped like a *Maghen David* (Star of David). The brass frames of each of these ritual objects bore round holes in which glasses of oil and wicks were inserted. Hung gracefully from the dining-room ceiling on brass chains, the *tirya* gave the impression of an oil-lamp chandelier. The *hanukkiya* was mounted on the wall.

At Passover the making of the matzahs on the premises of the Beth-el synagogue was supervised for kashrut by the Matzah Board. Flower remembers the matzahs being brought home from the synagogue in a cane matzah basket, the size of a small bathtub. The fragile and brittle matzahs, each about 16 inches in diameter, were piled high one on top of the other and placed in the basket. The basket was lined with a fresh cotton sheet. Once laden with matzahs, the corners of the sheet were drawn over the pile and bound with a knot. The matzah basket was brought home from the synagogue balanced atop a hand-drawn cart or rickshaw. This elaborate contraption was mounted with pulley and rope, and stored on the back verandah ceiling. It was ceremoniously lowered and raised each day by the servants to meet the daily matzah needs of the family.

Mary had five children, two of whom died as babies. She was very keen on giving her children a sound Jewish upbringing and an English education. Her home was run on strict Jewish lines, and rituals were observed meticulously. Mary lived by sets of rules she imposed on her life and her family in fairly rigid and uncompromising ways. Her two sons, Saleh (Charles) and Ezra Mir (Eric),[22] attended the Calcutta Boys' School, a Christian School where they paid fees, rather than the Talmud Torah, a free school for Jewish boys. This decision was made because the standard of education was higher at the former. Many Jewish boys attended this school, where they mixed freely with the Anglo-Indian boys who constituted the majority of the students. Flower was enrolled at the Jewish Girls'

School, which upheld a high standard of education under the able leadership of Miss Luddy.

Mary had household help who enabled her to juggle her home, children, and career. Bringing home his wages, Elias promptly handed it all over to Mary, who apportioned him some spending money and money to support his mother and siblings. Mary made all the financial decisions at home. As she disliked cooking, she relied on help from her sister's household when her own help was unavailable. When the cook was ill or returned to his village on leave, Mary promptly sent money enclosed in a note over to Matty's home, asking her to prepare and send over food. Mary had a full-time cook, a sweeper, and an ayah. Often, the rented apartments contained a few small rooms, the servants' quarters, which were located on the roof or in the basement of the building. Most often the ayahs lived with the family and slept on the floor of the child's room. Poorer Jews were employed to help with certain household or ritual chores, but they were never servants within the household. As I've already noted, the poorest Jews could rely on Jewish charities to help them support themselves and their families. The charities provided them with considerably higher amounts than the wages paid to a domestic servant. It was considered demeaning in the community for Jews to work as servants. While there were poor Jews, they were not as poor as the domestic work force in Calcutta. For example, even the poorer Jews could afford to have some domestic part-time help.

Jews always employed Muslim cooks because they shared many ritual practices, such as the eating of halal meat in accordance with Koranic laws. Muslims ate meat and therefore cooked it, but they did not eat pork and so there was no chance that they would bring it into Jewish kitchens. Muslim cooks knew that the halal meat of animals and birds killed in accordance with Islamic ritual was not to be brought into Jewish kitchens. They were trained to cook Jewish food as per kosher practices, such as separating milk and meat. Jews also preferred to hire Muslims because they would not bring 'idols' into Jewish homes. Mary ensured that her Muslim cook Karmalli learned kosher cooking, which she supervised with great attention. Karmalli was given money every day to buy the groceries and fresh produce from the market. The chickens were slaughtered by a shohet (ritual slaughterer). Chicken and fish were the primary meats eaten, though kosher red meat was prepared on high holidays when available. Mary's cook Karmalli later worked for my mother and reprimanded her when she did not follow kashrut or did not celebrate Jewish festivals with the 'right' kind of Jewish food preparations.

While the cooks working in Jewish homes cooked primarily Iraqi Jewish dishes, they also prepared food for themselves and the other servants. Typically, the servants gathered twice a day in the kitchen to eat a meal consisting of rice, lentils, vegetables, and chapatis. They also sometimes ate the leftover food given to them. Unlike the Anglo-Indians who emulated British culinary tastes, most Iraqi Jews preferred their own cuisine. Mary and her family, however, also enjoyed Indian spices. Often, traditional Iraqi dishes were modified and spiced because Baghdadi Jews had become used to the pungent flavours of Indian food.

The other household help included part-time workers like the jamedars (sweepers, who were usually Hindus from the untouchable community), dhobis (washermen, also from the Hindu community), and ayahs (who came from many communities, including Indian Christians and Nepalese). Handymen and message boys were employed by many members of the community and became part of the extended community.[23] Thus, in Jewish households, there were typically people from several faiths working together in close proximity.[24] This contrasted with Hindu or Muslim households, which for the most part employed servants of their own religion.

The sudden death of Mary's baby son, Mordecai (Dicky), at the age of two shook her to the core. He had gone to the park with his ayah. Upon returning home, they found he had contracted a rash. He developed a high fever and died the same night. After this tragic incident, Mary, blaming herself for his death, no longer entrusted her children to ayahs. Thereafter her younger children stayed in the home of her older sister, Matty, while she taught in the evenings. Simcha, by this time a widow, lived in the home of Matty, her eldest daughter. As was the custom among Baghdadi Jews in those days, Simcha helped run Matty's home and looked after her many grandchildren when they visited. If Simcha went to visit friends, she often took her grandchildren along with her.

After Dicky's death, Mary lost another baby in infancy. The deaths of her children induced a deep depression. She turned to religion and became even more rigid in her performance of religious ritual and duties. Her sister-in- law, Ruby, told me that Mary blamed herself for not listening to Farha, who told her to name the child after her deceased brother Aaron. Apparently Farha told Mary about a dream in which her brother Aaron had told her to pass his name on to her grandson. Mary did not believe Farha's dream and thought it was a trick to have her son named in memory of Farha's brother. Mary selected another name for her baby and later regretted it because she believed that her act of defiance brought bad luck to her baby.

Elias was less observant and superstitious than Mary. However, because of Mary's strong will, the house was strictly kosher and daily Jewish rituals were performed with precision. Elias went out to parties and was very gregarious, brought fun and laughter into the house, and was immensely popular. Although Mary was more introverted and serious, she did not mind when he went out on his own. Part of this was due to her strict observance of kashrut, which did not allow her to eat in any home that was not kosher. She did not want to offend people by not eating and so restricted her visits to the homes of Ruby and Matty.

Mary still enjoyed reading and the movies, which were perhaps a form of escape from her grief. During this period of her life, she went to the cinema two or three times a week. Though they were always very devoted to each other, Mary often went alone because Elias was working and did not share her passion for the movies. My mother recalls how her father often teased her mother when she returned from the movies: 'Whenever he asked her if she enjoyed a movie she answered in the superlative, so much so that he quipped about there being no movie that she did not like. Her response was that since the tickets were so reasonable she always got more than her money's worth.' It was not frowned upon in the community for middle-class women to go alone to the movies, so Mary did not have to seek anyone's approval or permission, which made the cinema an ideal dream space for her.

In the 1930s and 1940s the family moved several times in south Calcutta, where many members of the Jewish community had shifted over time. Mary always wanted to remain in close proximity to Matty and Ruby. Ruby told me that her brother Elias visited her each day, on his way to and from work. He stopped to greet her and to see if there was anything he could do to help her. She also remembers spending long hours with Mary, whom she loved like a sister. In addition to being close to her family, many of the cinemas were located in this area, making it even easier for her to indulge this passion. She became a regular customer at matinee shows. Her tastes remained the same, but her favourite stars were now

Bette Davis, Joan Crawford, Marlene Dietrich, Robert Taylor, James Stewart, and Gary Cooper. She saw *Gone with the Wind* again and again, and it remained her all-time favourite. Elias accompanied Mary only to musicals and comedies. He liked Betty Grable, Carmen Miranda, Abbott and Costello, and the Marx and Ritz Brothers.

By the late 1930s when Mary's children were in their teens, the family had acquired a phonograph and they enjoyed listening to records. Western records were freely available because HMV had built a new factory outside Calcutta. In fact, in the 1990s, records were still produced there and sent abroad for packaging. Before they were packed, a few of the records reached the Calcutta market and were bought up by aficionados. Many in the Jewish community developed a taste for both classical music and jazz and were up-to-date in Western musical styles. For instance, Matty's son Raz (Ezra) was an expert on jazz, swing, and big band music. Raz was a disc jockey with All India Radio, Calcutta in the 1940s with a show that aired twice a week.[25] Mary was an avid listener to All India Radio, which ran primarily Western programmes. Here again, she proved to be unlike the preceding generation of her family, who enjoyed Arabic music and dance performances. Mary and the next generation of Calcutta Jews had Western musical tastes. Only a few members of the Jewish community enjoyed Hindi music and gana bajana (song and music), as they called it.[26] They had no access to Arabic music except through traditional songs at wedding functions and community gatherings.

While Mary's social life revolved around her home, her extended family, community events, and the movies, the men in the family had much broader social worlds. Since Elias worked with Anglo-Indians, he often visited their clubs. Men gathered to drink, socialize, play cards and sports like cricket, football, and hockey in large canvas structures erected on the maidan. The Anglo-Indian clubs arranged dances in public halls like the Clem Browne Institute and the Rangers' Club at Christmas and New Year. While Anglo-Indian women accompanied their husbands to such events, Mary and other Jewish women rarely attended them.

Many ethnic communities in Calcutta had their own social clubs.[27] Some of the British clubs, like the Calcutta Swimming Club, were only open to the English and not even to other Europeans. All the European clubs were for Whites only, and they strictly enforced this membership policy. For example, the story goes that Sir David Ezra, one of the most prominent members of the Calcutta Jewish community, knighted by the British, applied for membership to the Bengal Club. He was refused membership. They had failed to take notice of the fact that he owned the land the club stood on and rented the property to them. He promptly demanded that the premises be vacated. The club members, when presented with this ultimatum, relented and extended him membership. He turned down their offer, renewed his rental agreement, and helped start the Calcutta Club. This club was open to people of all races and faiths. However, they drew firm class lines when it came to membership.[28]

The Judean Club was established in 1929 to provide cultural, social, and recreational programmes for Jewish adults. It was centrally located first in Kyd Street and later on Madge Lane (both close to the New Market, the Anglicized part of town), which by then had become a Jewish area. The Judean Club had a card room, a billiard room, a bar that served wine and snacks, and a community meeting hall, at which events like dances, weddings and political meetings were held. Older women attended the club primarily to play cards and talk; unmarried women welcomed this sanctioned space to meet young men from the community.[29]

In addition to playing cards and socializing at the Judean Club, Elias and other Jews enjoyed going to the horse races. This was a very popular sport among the Jews, even though the races were mostly held on the Sabbath. For the elite of Calcutta, attending the races in the member's enclosure was and still is a major social event. While Mary had no interest in the races, her sister Matty loved betting and following what was going on in the races, as did several other middle-class Jewish women. Since Matty could not go to the stands and place her own bets, she did it through Suffoo. Suffoo, a man from the community who did not hold a job, went to various homes to take bets. Whenever possible he stopped by on his rounds at mealtimes so that he would be invited to join in the meal.

The Abraham boys went to parties and dances, and were involved with boxing, weightlifting, hockey, and football. Since many of the social and sporting events were sponsored by their school, these functions were attended primarily by Anglo-Indian students and their sisters and friends, with whom Jewish boys mixed freely. Weightlifting was especially popular among Charles and Eric's cousins, who had started their own weight-lifting club—the Bob Hoffman Barbel Club—in their home in Royd Street. Their female cousins and sisters, on the other hand, were not allowed to go out freely. They spent their days at home in the company of Jewish friends and relatives. The girls played badminton, hockey, and basketball, and games such as hop-scotch, Monopoly, and jump rope. The Jewish community and Jewish events and festivals still marked the limits of their social world.

For the most part both men and women from the Jewish community eschewed politics at a time of intense political activity, even though Calcutta was the hotbed of political action for the nation. The period from the 1920s to the 1940s, when Mary was a young adult, witnessed many Indian women taking an increasing interest and active role in socio-political affairs. This was when the Civil Disobedience Movement was launched, capturing the imagination of the nation. Women participated in civil disobedience actions in large numbers. Many important women's associations were formed in this period, including the Indian Federation of University Women's Association, Women's India Association, the Calcutta branch of the All India Women's Conference, and All Bengal Women's Union. The early twentieth century also saw many Indian women involved in revolutionary political activities. Important laws were passed, like the women's right to vote, due to the political efforts of women.[30]

While all this was happening in Calcutta, right at the doorstep of the Jewish community, Mary did not consider it to be her business and was very comfortable with the compartmentalization between the Jews and 'the others.' The events were clearly beyond her Jewish world. Moreover, in the 1930s and 1940s, the nationalist movement was becoming increasingly identified with Hindu culture. Whereas Muslims contested the increasing Hinduization and eventually called for a separate state (Pakistan), the Jewish community was too small to have a significant voice and presence. They did not identify with the Hindus or the Muslims and did not consider themselves Indians. Most Jews just did not get involved in local politics, though they were nervous about what an India without British rule would mean for them. Though the forces of nationalism were going to fundamentally restructure her world, Mary was mostly interested in Jewish religious matters and in community affairs. Her world outside the community was that of Hollywood movies and British books. Like most of the community, she continued with her life, choosing to be completely uninvolved or neutral in political events till forced to take a position.

In the early 1940s Mary did cross from her Jewish and Anglo-oriented world into an Indian world on a regular basis. She found lucrative employment in the homes of a few wealthy Marwari families. This business community from Rajasthan had moved to Calcutta in the 1830s due to commercial opportunities. By the late nineteenth century they retained a hold on inter-regional money circulation and the flow of imported goods and spices.[31] By the late twentieth century they became one of the most influential and wealthy communities in the city and the country. Today, a handful of large Marwari families like the Birlas, Modis, and Goenkas dominate India's financial and industrial sectors. Several of these families, including the Birlas, started to build their commercial and industrial empires in Calcutta in the late nineteenth and early twentieth century. As the Marwari community prospered, the more successful amongst them sought to make their wives familiar with Western ways and with the English language. These wealthy Marwari families had well-off Jewish friends and business colleagues who recommended Mary—who had taught their children—as a good teacher. Mary went to teach the women of these joint family households how to knit, crochet, and speak English. She introduced Ruby to this work as well. Both Mary and Ruby taught Marwari women the basic social skills, such as the English language, social customs, and etiquette that they needed to be successful in Calcutta's cosmopolitan society.[32] While spending the days with the women, Mary also taught the preschool children enough English to enable them to gain admittance into English-medium schools.

Mary worked in the homes of the leading Marwaris of Calcutta, including the Kejriwals and the Jalans. They sent a chauffeur-driven car each morning to pick her up from Tottee Lane. She was dropped home in the late afternoon. In addition to her wages her students showered her with gifts—perfumes, clothing, jewellery—and treated her with great respect. In the 1950s and 1960s when Ruby moved to London, she chaperoned her former students to see the sights. She took them on outings to the West End and helped them in their shopping expeditions. Ruby was rewarded handsomely for her services. Now, at the age of ninety, she still keeps in touch with a few of them and remembers them fondly.

The exposure to Indian homes and culture through her work with Marwari women made Mary aware that there were other worlds beyond her Jewish world in Calcutta. She became more familiar with Indian ways, got to sample many more Indian dishes, and became somewhat familiar with their culture. However, she set the terms of her engagement with

Indianness. She retained her distance and wanted it that way. Mary considered herself different from Indians and from the British as well. There were characteristics that she clearly admired—the respect for teachers and learning, as well as the generosity she experienced. She looked up to the British but did not see British culture as superior to her Jewish culture, rather, she felt that there was much to learn from British culture that did not contradict her own. And although she differentiated herself from Indians and Indianness, it is hard to tell whether she actively thought of Indians as inferior or just different.

Certainly, Mary's schooling and the broader cultural environment during the heyday of British imperialism in the early twentieth century upheld the belief in English superiority and projected Orientalist notions of 'inferior cultures'.[33] The hierarchy saw British and Europeans at the apex of the social pyramid along with a few members from other communities; Anglo-Indians, Jews, and Parsis were predominantly in the middle tiers; and the 'natives', for the most part but with many exceptions, were at the bottom. Of course, class issues intersected the pyramid, placing some natives (such as Indian royalty) on the top tier of the pyramid, along with a few members of other communities. Because of Jewish charities and British race privilege, which favoured the Jews by giving them a quasi-European status, poorer Jews like Mary were able to access many middle-class privileges despite their lower economic status. As a result of her schooling and the dominant social norms of the time, Mary no doubt imbibed and maintained this sense of racial hierarchy throughout her life. And yet it remains hard to gauge whether for Mary and other Calcutta Jews of her generation, this differentiation from Indians and Indianness was born out of an 'intrinsic' racism or from a fear of being besieged by the India around them.[34] What is clear is that the Calcutta Jews were always engaged in a selective process regarding which parts of India and Indian culture to adopt and which ones to keep at bay. Here, again, while Mary crossed an invisible border by going into Indian homes and becoming part of their households, she took her borders with her. It is important to underline that these were all internal borders that were constantly being drawn and redrawn in order to maintain difference and distance.

For instance, although Mary adopted Western clothes along with much of Western culture which she associated with being modern and forward-looking, Mary never even considered wearing Indian clothing. Wearing Indian clothes was seen as a shameful betrayal in the Jewish community, tantamount to identifying with India and Indianness. Yet Mary was quite comfortable speaking in Hindustani and eating Indian food at home—more private acts which did not mark her publicly. She was particular about how she looked and developed a distinct sense of fashion. While the wealthy pored over French and European dress magazines, ordered dresses from abroad, or had their clothes made by European dress-makers in Calcutta, Mary selected the fabric, buttons, lace, and other trimmings (almost all of which were imported from England), to be sewn by local (typically Muslim) durzees who artfully imitated the styles in the magazines. Always unassuming, Mary wore sober colours and looked a lot older than her age.

It is interesting to note that the conservative Marwari community, which maintained strict mores for its women, was comfortable having Jewish women spend all day at home teaching its wives and daughters. Since women like Mary were religiously observant, essentially conservative, and stayed socially within the confines of their own community, they were warmly received. Because Mary was so sober and conservative, she was particularly suited for this job. And because Mary mixed only with women and could eat vegetarian (and thus kosher) food, this was a safe environment for her and one in which she felt comfortable and at ease in turn. Marwaris rarely hired Anglo-Indian women in these roles, perhaps because they were perceived as more Western and outgoing. Anglo-Indians may have been perceived as too Western or too British, and maybe even too White, for Marwaris to feel at ease with them. Here again it was the ambiguous status of the Jews, as opposed to the Anglo-Indian who identified with the British, that worked to Mary's personal advantage. Unlike the Baghdadi Jews, the Anglo-Indians always referred to England as 'home'. During the time the Jews lived in Calcutta, they did not consider their home to be somewhere else, except that in a spiritual sense Israel was a home. Even now, as Baghdadi Jews have left Calcutta for many other parts of the world, they reminisce fondly about their childhoods and their lives in Calcutta.

The Second World War forever shattered the life Mary led and fundamentally altered the moorings of the Calcutta Jewish community. One of the immediate changes ushered in by the War was that the community came in direct contact with Jews from other parts of the world. For example, there were British and American Jewish servicemen stationed in Calcutta and Southeast Asia in relatively large numbers. These young men attended the local synagogues and were accorded hospitality by the Judean

Club and by members of the community. Because the club could not extend hospitality to all the servicemen, it requested Jewish families to host them for Sabbath and festivals. Mary, however, always cautious and conservative in disposition, did not extend them this hospitality. She had a young daughter at home and did not want her exposed to their more liberal ways. It was disconcerting for Mary to see some of the Calcutta Jewish girls marrying Jews from faraway places and different traditions.

In 1942 Mary and her extended family, along with other Jewish families, were evacuated to Delhi for five months. Thus, she went to Delhi along with her mother, Simcha, her mother-in-law, Farha, her sister-in-law, Ruby, and their children, to avoid the Japanese air raids on Calcutta. This evacuation was very difficult for Mary because there was no Baghdadi community in Delhi, which left her unable to participate in communal religious and social activities. This was the only time in her life that she went to a place where she was not part of Jewish community life. It was an alienating experience. Mary had never studied Indian history because it was not part of the British school curriculum in India, and so Delhi and its rich history were not familiar to her. She never used the opportunity to explore the city, though it was probably her first time out of Calcutta. To her Delhi only had utilitarian value—it was an interim phase till she and her family could return to the bosom of their own community. When Mary and her family returned to Calcutta to celebrate the Jewish high holidays (Roshashanah, the Jewish New Year, and Yom Kippur), they decided not to return to Delhi.

After the War Mary and most of the Jews steered clear of politics and were neutral in the Hindu-Muslim riots that rocked Calcutta and the rest of India. By and large the community remained loyal British subjects and were fearful of the future and what it might bring. However, once India gained its independence in 1947, Calcutta Jewry participated in ceremonies celebrating the inauguration of India as a republic, including a function held at the Judean Club, followed by special prayers at Maghen David Synagogue. The leading Calcutta Jewish firm of B. N. Elias and Co. honoured the occasion with a flag-hoisting ceremony. While Jews participated in Indian elections and most accepted Indian citizenship, they were unsure of their economic future in India. This, together with the opening up of immigration possibilities to England, Israel, and Australia, as well as the marriage of Jewish girls to American servicemen, led many to consider emigrating. Family members often left to join the initial few who emigrated. This emigration from an already small community made it very difficult to sustain community life in Calcutta.

During the five years after independence, each person living in India could make the decision to be British or Indian and accordingly get the necessary passport and go to the country selected. Many Indians, several from India's minority communities, opted for British nationality. They had to raise enough money to pay for their passage to start new lives in England. As part of a wave of Jewish emigration out of India on the eve of India's independence in 1947, Mary's elder son Charles applied for a visa to Australia when the White Australia Policy was in force. This policy only extended the 'privilege' of emigration to Anglo-Indians, Armenians, Jews, and a few Parsis.[35] After World War II, Australia had opened up its immigration policy because some politicians believed that Australia required a larger population to protect itself in case of war. Arthur Calwell, the Labour Government's Minister for Immigration coined the phrase 'Populate or Perish' to make Australians accept the new policy. Immigration was extended to Southern Europeans but Australia drew the line when it came to including Asian, African, and Middle-Eastern immigrants. At first, in the mid-1940s, Middle-Eastern Jews were not eligible to enter Australia. However, a few years later several Armenians, Anglo-Indians, Jews, and Parsis emigrated to Australia. These applicants, including Charles, had to be certified as having no Indian blood in order to be considered for immigration. Thus, while Jews were considered 'Whiter' in India, their degree of Whiteness had to be approved to pass as sufficiently 'White' in Australia.

Australia distinguished between 'White, European' Jews and 'coloured, Asiatic Jews'. Given the adherence to a 'Whiteness' policy, Ashkenazi Jews were privileged over Asiatic Jews, whereas previously all Jews fell under the same category. In the first implementation of this policy, Jews from the Middle East were considered to be 'Asian' and thereby not allowed into Australia.[36] In 1951, this policy gave way to the '75 percent European blood' policy for Asian applicants. In this racist schema anything 'more than 25% makes a person look too colored—too Asian— and suggests their unassimilability.'[37] Thenceforth judgments on Sephardic immigration applications were made according to a visual inspection of the applicant. Charles passed this visual inspection and was granted a visa.[38] By 1954 the '75 percent' rule was adhered to less strictly, which led to an increased number of Indian, Egyptian, Iraqi, and other Oriental Jews entering Australia.

When Charles left India, he was assisted by a relative, Mrs Gubbay, who had left for Australia with her husband some twenty years earlier. Charles stayed with the Gubbays till he established himself—once again the Baghdadi community network proved invaluable in making a new 'home'. Five years later, Charles married an Australian Jewish (Ashkenazi) woman, and Mary and Elias visited Australia for the wedding. Two years later (1955), the Abrahams emigrated to Sydney, one of the places where the first wave of Jews from Calcutta to Australia had settled. Elias, being born in Singapore, a Crown colony, was a British citizen. In imperial eyes this designation was of higher status than a British subject. This hierarchy worked in their favour, making it easier for them to emigrate to Australia. Although members of the community who had recently emigrated welcomed the Abrahams, Mary found Australia an alien place. Her sojourn there was extremely short-lived due to the unexpected death of Elias. Within a year of leaving Calcutta, he died one night of a sudden heart attack. Mary was devastated by his death and returned to Calcutta, where she mourned him for many years.

On her return Mary began living in her daughter Flower's home. Though not observant, Flower made her home kosher so Mary could live with her. Still, Mary did not feel comfortable in this non-religious environment and so rented a place close to the Shaare Rason synagogue, which she had previously attended but which was not within walking distance of Flower's home. Mary gave up going to the movies, became vegetarian, and turned more intensely to religion. Her faith intensified with each major loss and setback in her life, and in times of grief she found great solace and refuge in prayer and in Judaism. Thus, during this period in her life, she attended classes in Hebrew and Jewish studies by Rabbi Ezekiel Musleah, who had returned from studying in the Jewish theological seminary in New York. She chanted a portion of the psalms each day in order to complete the entire book of 150 psalms each week. She spent a lot of time reading her prayers, and her psalm book was always near at hand. She strictly followed the letter of the law and taught us grandchildren the prayers as well as Jewish religious values and customs. She gave to religious charities both in India and elsewhere and was active in Jewish community affairs. She sent money to the Porath Yosef Yeshiva, a Sephardic yeshiva in Jerusalem, and to Rabbi Meir bal Hanes, the kabbalist (person who practices Jewish mysticism), also in Jerusalem, because she had a lifelong interest in Jewish mysticism.

In 1960, when Flower went on an extended trip with her children to London, Mary accompanied the family. In London, she went to visit the royal sites and the Tower of London. She enjoyed visiting the English places she had grown up imagining from novels, the cinema, newsreels, and popular songs. While her daughter and her grandchildren returned to Calcutta as planned, Mary decided to stay on in London. In the early 1960s Golders Green had become home to a large Iraqi community. Baghdadi Jews from Shanghai, Burma, India, and Singapore had settled there. In fact, there were more Calcutta Jews living in Golders Green than in Calcutta. These Jews lived close to each other and mostly socialized with one another. Mary also had close family in London, including her son Eric and her sister-in-law, Ruby. Mary made a fresh start for herself in Golders Green. She attended the synagogue, where Sephardic services were held in Iraqi Jewish style. It was here that she met up with the Shanghai branch of her family, which she had not met before. It turned out that her cousin (Simcha's brother's son) was the hazan of the Golders Green synagogue. With the money from Elias's pension she was able to rent a room and provide for herself. Her simple lifestyle, the proximity of Ruby, and the emotional and spiritual support of the Iraqi community made London 'home' for a few years.

While living in London, Mary visited the Holy Land and met relatives and friends. She attempted to see if she could make a life for herself in Israel. She tried to learn modern Hebrew but at her age found it too difficult. Her Hebrew pronunciation was attuned to the biblical articulation in which she was fluent. The different style of modern Hebrew was like a new language. Her desire to live in Israel was thwarted in several ways. She really wanted to join a religious kibbutz (a cooperative built on socialist principles), for at this point in her life she was searching for a place where she could live simply, eat kosher food, and fulfill her religious obligations. Mary was not accepted as a member of a kibbutz because she was in her mid-sixties and would be entering without a family.[39] My mother told me about a poignant letter she received from Mary during this period. On a visit to members of Elias's family in Eilat, Mary happened to visit a prison. She was very impressed with what she saw and wrote that it was peaceful, quiet, and air-conditioned, with a view of the sea. To top it all, the prison inmates were served kosher food. She concluded the letter with a half-serious question: 'Do you think if I committed a crime I could stay here for the rest of my life?' Her letter saddens me and underlines her desperate yet fruitless search for a place to live in Israel. Because she could not find a way to live in Israel and was still unable to accept her husband's sudden death, Mary returned to London. Soon after, she was offered a job in Calcutta as the superintendent of the Jewish Girls' School hostel.

In 1966, at the age of sixty-five, Mary returned to Calcutta to run the hostel. A large two-storey mansion located on the grounds of the Jewish Girls' School in the heart of south Calcutta, it provided a home for the poorer Jewish girls attending the school on scholarships. Mary lived with the girls in the hostel and was a surrogate mother to them. She had a spacious room and attached bathroom, and there were four other large dormitory-style rooms that the girls shared on the second floor of the building. There was a big hall with a piano where the girls gathered to socialize and a dining room where they all ate together. There were large grounds where the girls played. Mary presided over the meals and supervised the running of the kitchen. She identified with the hostel girls, for she too had come from a humble background. It was her school experience that had moulded her character and provided her with opportunities that shaped her life, and she wanted to extend this opportunity to them. Daily she took it upon herself to provide for their material, spiritual, educational, and emotional needs. She was very strict, and watched over their studies, saw to their clothing, counselled them, and went to great lengths to inspect each vegetable they ate before it was cooked by the domestic help to ensure that halachic laws were upheld. In the evenings she helped the girls with their homework and sang and talked with them. She made sure that not a day went by without prayers.

When necessary, she intervened with parents on behalf of the girls. Together with Miss Luddy, she was instrumental in arranging for many of the hostel girls to emigrate to Israel. The Jewish Agency was supporting Jews who wished to make aliyah (emigration to Israel), but many of the girls' families could not afford the application fees. Mary helped raise the money and consequently many of these young women were able to make better lives for themselves in Israel. Through her actions she ensured that the values of the community were passed on and that opportunities were made available to even the poorest members of the community. Although she tried to sustain community life among the few Jewish girls left, she was at the same time presiding over the demise of the community by helping the girls in the hostel to leave and start new Jewish lives elsewhere.

This must have been doubly painful to her because Israeli society had deemed her too old to make a life there. She wanted these girls to make the move when they were still young, so that they could establish themselves in Jewish worlds that no longer existed in Calcutta.

In addition to her work at the hostel, Mary was involved in many other Jewish community affairs. She visited the older members of the dwindling community and served on the Oseh Haised Board (Jewish Burial Board). She attended burials and washed the bodies of the women, preparing them for burial. This was considered a very important mitzvah.[40] She knitted and crocheted *kippas* (skull caps) for the members of the community and helped young boys prepare for their bar mitzvahs. She taught her grandchildren to read Hebrew and worked with us on our prayers. While she always believed in dreams and was of a mystical bent, during this period of her life she read further and studied gematriya and kabbala and interpreted dreams. Her dreams were prophetic and typically had to do with community and family affairs. For example, many years later while in Israel she dreamt of two talits (prayer shawls) and two carriages and correctly predicted that two of her granddaughters would have baby boys within the year. Many of her dreams had to do with predicting births and deaths of family and community members. At every level of her being, even in her subconscious, she was deeply engaged with the community and its continuation.

Throughout the 1970s the Calcutta Jewish community dwindled further. Most of Mary's contemporaries and relatives had either died or left India. Religious facilities fell to a low ebb, and the synagogues employed inept readers, who would have previously been employed as minyan men, to read the services. The Jewish Girls' School was forced by the new government regulations to admit non-Jewish students. It was against this backdrop of religious community disintegration that Mary heeded her sister-in-law Ruby's persistent plea to join her in London. Ruby's husband had died and she wanted to be close to Mary in their waning years. Ruby had found out that, because Mary was a British citizen and of retirement age, she was eligible for a small pension from the British government. With a guarantee of some financial security, Mary decided to return to London.

Mary worked as a companion in the home of an older English Jewish woman in Golders Green, where she received a room in exchange. She picked up the threads of her life as part of the Iraqi community. She remained close to Ruby, continued teaching boys their bar mitzvah prayers, and took part again in Iraqi community life. When her daughter, Flower, divorced and moved to Israel, she invited Mary to come and live with her in Jerusalem. This was a dream come true for Mary: a chance to live in the Holy City. She had long nursed a secret longing to die in Israel and be buried on the Mount of Olives. And so, at the age of seventy-seven, Mary went to Israel, in 1978.

In Jerusalem, Mary immediately re-established contact with members of her family who had emigrated to Israel. She was extremely close all her life to her older sister, Matty, who had left Calcutta to live with her daughter, Tillie, and Tillie's family when they emigrated to Israel. Mary spent many days and most weekends with Matty in Tel Aviv. The long weekend visits to Matty's home were deeply satisfying. They spent much of their time reminiscing about the good old days in Calcutta, talking about their children, grandchildren, and relatives who were spread across the globe. Because Mary wrote profusely to relatives and friends all over the world, she filled Matty in on community news. Always more open-minded, Matty was much more modern than Mary in her outlook on life. Puffing on her cigarette, she explained to Mary that the world was changing and emphasized the necessity of keeping up with the times. With her strong sense of humour, Matty was among the few people who made Mary laugh. Once, concerned that Matty's son was still not married, Mary asked why her son was still a bachelor and yet continued to have many girlfriends. Matty answered: 'Mary, why do you want him to make only one woman happy? This way he can make so many women happy.'

Mary attended the Sephardic synagogue in Kiryat Moshe, a few blocks from where she lived. She visited Rachel's tomb outside Jerusalem. Mary loved visiting the religious sites, especially on high holidays. Particularly significant for her was attending the Hanukkah ceremonies at the Western Wall, where giant urns are lit for each day of the festival and prayers are recited each night in different traditional melodies. Despite the inspirational aspects of Jewish life, Mary was deeply disillusioned and alienated—everyday life in Israel did not resonate with the Holy Land she had imagined for herself. She was too rigid in her beliefs to conform to religious norms in Israel, predominantly derived from Ashkenazi traditions. Among many other things, she was unfamiliar with laws of shmeetah (keeping the fields fallow in the seventh year), found the concept of parve foods (neither milky nor meaty) confusing, and the belief that religious women should cover their hair very alien. Her conservative dresses had sleeves below the elbow and she would wear a *kippa* to say her prayers and attend shul. However, although she was deeply religious, Mary did not cover her hair. This was frowned upon by the more orthodox Ashkenazi Jews, who conform to a strict style of dress. Even Sephardic services differed from the Baghdadi services to which she was accustomed. Thus, while she wanted to end her life in the Holy Land, Israel was never 'home' to her. It is ironic that in the heart of the Jewish 'homeland' she should feel so out of place. However, it was not just Judaism that provided her with a sense of community, but a particular practice of Judaism, a mindset and lifestyle that was essential for her to feel as though she belonged.

Mary spent her life building family and community in a diasporic context even as the continuation of the community as she knew it was seriously threatened. She was at once rooted and rootless in a deterritorialized community: 'home' was not a consistent geographic space; rather, it was a shifting site. As the locus of the community shifted, so did she. Calcutta, or, more specifically, the Jewish community in Calcutta, was her 'home' for most of her life. That was the only Calcutta she knew and, when there was no Jewish community left, she felt compelled to leave the city in search of home. Mary did not see herself as a citizen of any particular place and kept her ties to many places; her form and practice of Judaism defined and sustained her. Born in India, she could return to India to live and work whenever she wanted. Her lack of Indian citizenship did not exclude her from any benefits except the right to vote. Her status as a Jew and her husband's British citizen status gave them preference in emigrating to Australia. On this basis, too, she was able to emigrate to Britain with a small pension. Her Jewish status meant she could emigrate to Israel where she wanted to be buried. Because Mary was Jewish, her racial categorization was ambiguous and changed as definitions of 'Whiteness', 'British subject' versus 'British citizen', and Jewish status changed to meet imperial political and racial agendas in imperial England and Australia, where identity is based on racial categorization. She was able to use her ambiguous racial and national status to advantage and accrued greater mobility and financial benefits because of it.

For much of her later life 'home' was a room set in an unfamiliar and often alien place, but it was a place from which she could continue to be part of her community, remain close to her family members, and perform her religious duties in the manner to which she was accustomed. I remember many rooms where my grandmother lived in Calcutta, London, and then in Jerusalem. While the large room in the Jewish Girls' School hostel in Calcutta was bright and airy, with high ceilings, and her rooms in London and Jerusalem were very small with barely enough space for a bed and chair, they all had felt similar—sparsely furnished, very clean, and exactingly neat. An opened prayer book always lay on a table or shelf, together with a book of psalms and some novels. I remember a radio too. When she was not reading her prayers or carrying out daily chores, she tuned in and hummed along to popular songs while her crochet or knitting needles clicked continuously.

Ironically, of all the places in which she lived, Israel was the most alien to her. There, Sephardic Jews and their customs were often looked down upon as ignorant and superstitious. They did not follow the letter of the law as interpreted by Ashkenazi Jews. Moreover, Mary's notions of what life was and should be in the Holy Land were different from the reality of Israel in the 1980s. She had sought out Israel because to her it was a religious and holy place, and she was uncomfortable with Israeli secular life.

In her last years Mary became preoccupied with her own death and the arrangements that she needed to make for it. Because she had come to Jerusalem to die, she had bought burial insurance from London. However, to her dismay, she had learned that Jews who lived and died in Jerusalem were buried there automatically at no cost. The idea of having a free burial upset her terribly, for she had strong Dickensian views on the subject. In her eyes a free grave was tantamount to a 'pauper's grave'. She extracted a promise from her daughter, Flower, that the burial insurance would be used to pay for her grave. Since Mary had selected a particular site for the grave she was able to pay for it. Her wish to be buried on the Mount of Olives was fulfilled. This is a most auspicious site, for, when the Messiah comes, and the dead are supposed to rise, it is said that those who are buried on the Mount will be the first to follow Him through the Gate of the Old City.

In 1980 Mary had a stroke. Because she was paralysed, it was necessary for her to be moved to a home for the disabled in Ramleh. Ruby and Matty came to be with her and help nurse her, and many other relatives visited her frequently. At Ramleh she met up with a friend from the Calcutta community who suffered from a broken hip but could move around in a wheel chair. She took special care of Mary and kept her company at the home. When Mary died a few months later, Flower carried out her careful instructions and she was buried on the Mount of Olives. Her burial ceremony in Jerusalem was attended by Flower and her children, Mary's son Eric who came from London, her sister Matty and all her nieces and nephews who lived in Israel. Many members of the Iraqi Jewish community paid their respects as well. During that week of shiva (mourning), women from the Jewish Girls' School and hostel, where she had taught and worked for so many years, came to mourn her death. To be surrounded by family and community seems to me a fitting end to Mary's life. Her resting place on the Mount of Olives marks the culmination of her spiritual yearning. The Golden Gate stands opposite her grave.

Mary reworked and reinscribed cultural forms and traditions from Baghdad, India and England to form a somewhat seamless tapestry that was only richer for the multiple strands it embodied. Her lifestyle and value system defies notions of cultural purity. She 'encoded practices of accommodation with, as well as resistance to, host countries and their norms.'[41] For example, while she was very comfortable in India, she chose not to be part of it. However, this did not stop her from adopting and adapting parts of India and Indian culture to suit her own needs, and she was very comfortable doing this as she was living in Calcutta. When she left India, she, along with her friends and relatives, recalled their past with great fondness and nostalgia.

In Australia, England and Israel, countries where she later resided, she anchored herself in the life of the Baghdadi Jewish community, which was her 'home'. The familiar travel circuits in which Iraqi Jews were involved made her feel that though she had travelled to a distant place her 'home', the community, remained the same. In each of these places there were people she knew who shared religious customs, foods and worldviews. Till Mary's death this imagined community was very much intact.

In Calcutta and in the other Iraqi community settings in England, Australia and Israel she did not venture out much into the dominant societies that surrounded her. This underlines how 'home' can be set in an alien landscape. The physical and social landscape in which her home existed was almost incidental to her, so long as the outside world and events did not impinge upon or disrupt her pattern of life. Mary's profession, that of a teacher, was a skill that could be transferred and continued in different settings.

This account of Mary's life unsettles notions that cultural flows and patterns aligned themselves neatly with national borders or nation states. While today this flow of ideas across borders is understood as a post-modern phenomenon, her life demonstrates that this is nothing new but part of her community's long history. So many members of the Baghdadi Jewish community moved through porous borders for centuries while taking their own borders with them. As they moved, they recreated their communities and traditions in very diverse settings. They created very hybrid cultural forms, even while the Sephardic Jewish core remained constant. Thus, it was perfectly natural for my grandmother to say her *brachot*, settle down to eat a kosher meal of Indian food, listen to Western popular music after her meal, and to curl up in the cool of her room in the hot Calcutta afternoons with a British novel. Although she might be regarded as an example of 'hybridity', Mary did not feel as though she was mixing cultures nor did she feel fragmented. I contend that the term 'multilocationality' across geographical, cultural and psychic boundaries captures her sentiments more accurately than 'displacement'. She effortlessly seemed to face in several different directions at once.

Mary's Baghdadi Jewish life, lying between Indian and English life, though not in the interstices, has been erased from colonial histories. The idea of an Englishwoman as a person with rights, powers and capabilities emerged from contrasts with Asian and Middle-Eastern women, who were perceived by Englishwomen in the nineteenth century in an undifferentiated manner. They were viewed as impoverished and purdah-clad bodies with no minds, rights and freedoms—the antithesis of the free thinking British woman. Consequently they were treated with disdain. Such false dichotomies created for colonial purposes made the lives of women like Mary, who did not fit these either/or categories, almost invisible.[42] The women in Mary's family, by moving from Iraq to British India, were able to carve out new social and economic spaces for themselves that were closed to their forebears. This move gave them tremendous social and economic mobility.

Mary, while from a very poor Jewish background, had many rights and freedoms. She acquired an education, pursued her career, and supported herself through much of her life. Contrary to British depictions of Asian women, her successful bid for a career mirrored what several progressive Indian women in India were doing at this time. For the most part, though, the worlds of Mary and other Indian women pursuing their education and careers did not intersect, nor did she come into direct contact with British women in India, who occupied a rarefied social space. Women in each of these communities, while pursuing educational and career goals, did so in their separate social and cultural spaces.

Mary's life, which is that of an 'ordinary' Jewish woman, was in many ways very 'extraordinary' given the times, the place, and the conservative community from which she came. She was able to have a fulfilling personal and professional life, to choose where she wanted to live and be buried, and to devote herself to her religion and to the performance of community activities. Through her work in Jewish education and in the hostel, she was able to create many opportunities and impact upon the lives of many Jewish girls while doing what was meaningful and important to her.

This narrative shows how Mary's life consisted of making the most of opportunities and improving her lot through an on-going process of selection and rejection. She did this without a broader social and political consciousness. She had a strong sense of duty to her family, her religion and her community that determined the choices that she made. The Iraqi society from whence she came was, when rooted in a different place, amenable to change and adaptation in order to thrive in a new environment. For women of this diaspora community, the shift from Baghdad to Calcutta brought considerably greater freedom. Women were able to choose more liberating roles because Calcutta, an important colonial city, was more outward looking and modern in its cultural orientation than Baghdad. Mary did not face any resistance as she responded to new educational and career opportunities. As a middle-class woman living in India she was able to afford household help. This meant that she could pursue her career and enjoy her leisure by going to the movies or spending her time in community and religious activities.

Thus I would argue that Mary did in fact make the most of her complex and flexible positioning. She turned necessity into opportunity and (for the most part) gained rather than lost in this process. Salman Rushdie expresses this sentiment eloquently: 'It is normally supposed that something always gets lost in translation; I cling, obstinately, to the notion that something can also be gained.'[43] My grandmother seemed to have used her ambivalent status to seize new opportunities for advancement and to gain greater social and economic mobility. However, Mary never did find a place that she could unequivocally call home, except for that of the shifting Baghdadi community. Perhaps her burial space on the Mount of Olives was the imagined home, part of that Jewish mythology to which she clung, that anchored her through all her journeys, that she longed for and turned to through all her tribulations. Thus it was an appropriate resting place, one she attained only when she died.

Notes

Flyleaf: Portrait of Mary

1 Musleah, *On the Banks of the Ganga*, p. 190

2 David Sassoon fled the persecution of Daud Pasha in the 1820s and settled in Bombay. He became fabulously wealthy dealing in textiles. His second wife was Farha (Flora) Hayeem, whom he married in Baghdad before he came to settle in Bombay. Farha, in Baghdad, wore purdah and even in India she rarely ventured out of doors except to attend the synagogue or to visit the Jewish poor. She was the daughter of a merchant and bibliophile who later fled to Calcutta. Farha bore David eight children. She has been described as a 'gentle matriarch' piously devoted to the minutiae of household ritual. Her son Solomon married the legendary Flora Sassoon, known for her business acumen and philanthropy, after whom the famous Flora Fountain in Bombay was named. For more information on the Sassoons see Jackson, *The Sassoons*.

3 Most Jewish women supervised their own households to ensure that halacha (religious law) was maintained.

4 From the early twentieth century, as Jewish firms grew, they hired members of the community, making observance and employment less problematic. Till then, as the more wealthy in the community respected religious duties, Jewish charities were established to support men whose religious duties barred them from getting regular jobs.

5 There were several Jewish charities operating at the end of the nineteenth century. At the turn of the century there was an attempt to set up a central Jewish fund to provide assistance to deserving and respectable Jews and to widows and children. In 1911 the Jewish Charitable Fund, supported by the richer members of the community, was established. See Musleah, *On the Banks of the Ganga*, p. 109.

6 In 1860 Mrs Ewart, a Scottish missionary, opened her school for girls. See Tilottama Tharoor (ed.), *Naari* (Calcutta: Ladies' Study Group, 1990), p. 10. This was forty years after the first school for girls, the

Juvenile School, was started in Calcutta by Christian missionaries in 1820. The Bethune School for girls was founded in 1849 under the patronage of Drinkwater Bethune, Dakshinaranjan Mukherjee, Ramgopal Ghosh, Madanmohan Tarkalankar and others from the Bengali bhadralok community. After the establishment of the Bethune School numerous girls' schools were established in other parts of the city, such as Victoria College (1882), and Brahmo Balika Sikshalaya (1890). See Tharoor, *Naari*, p. 45. Before the turn of the century there were many girls' schools in Calcutta.

7 Talmud Torah, the Jewish school for boys, was founded after Jewish Girls' School on April 5, 1881. Whereas initially the Jewish Girls' and Infants' School admitted boys between the ages of eight and ten, later the boys were moved to separate premises under the same management, forming the Jewish Boys' School. See Musleah, *On the Banks of the Ganga*, p. 277.

8 Ibid., p. 275.

9 Gauri Viswanathan, 'Currying Favor: The Politics of British Educational and Cultural Policy in India, 1813–1854', in Anne McClintock et al (ed.), *Dangerous Liaisons* (Minneapolis: Minnesota University Press, 1997), p. 128.

10 In this way Miriam transfers value to the colonial power. S. Shankar in *Textual Traffic: Colonialisms, Modernity and the Economy of the Text* (New York: State University of New York, 2001) discusses the economy of the text to illustrate the way in which values are transferred from the peripheries to the centre. Whereas his argument is made in the context of the text, the notion of the transfer of values is useful to analyse the ways in which colonial values were upheld in the colonies.

11 I obtained this information from an interview with Ramah Musleah who was a student in the school, and eight years junior to Mary. She later taught at the Jewish Girls' School till she retired, in her seventies.

12 During her lifetime and at her death in London there were numerous occasions when she was honoured. Her students from all over Britain and from as far away as the United States and Canada came to pay their respects to her.

13 During my discussions in Calcutta with Maggie Meyer, who was from a very wealthy Jewish family and only a decade younger than Mary, she told me that she went to finishing school in the thirties in Brighton and

was accompanied there by her mother. She was sent thereafter to study dress-making and fashion design in France. At her father's home, Europeans and elite Indians alike were entertained. She had European, Marwari and Bengali friends. One of her sisters, Mozelle, married the Prince of Murshidabad though their marriage was disapproved of by her family.

14 Mary's school reports from the Jewish Girls' School in 1912 and 1913 tell us that she received second prize in tunnach (Bible). Her brother was among the boys with 100% synagogue attendance (1912). In the 1913 report, Mary got the first prize in standard three as well as the writing prize. Her brother still maintained his 100% attendance in synagogue and even Mary is mentioned for her regular attendance.

15 Kathy Peiss in *Cheap Amusements: Working Women and Leisure in Turn-of-the-Century New York* (Philadelphia: Temple University Press, 1986), discusses how movies were a popular form of entertainment for working-class women in New York for very much the same reasons—affordability. She also discusses how the early movies expressed and legitimized a heterosocial culture, and how this form of entertainment could easily be incorporated into the world and lives of married women.

16 The film scene in India, as elsewhere at the turn of the century, was extremely international. While France was the leading source of films, American, Italian, English, Danish and German films competed for a share of the Indian market. In the next decade Indian films were being made as well. However, with the advent of the war in 1914, film production almost stopped in France and Italy, and British production was stifled with scarcities and restrictions, while German studios were isolated, which gave American films a huge lead in the market. By 1926-27 then, 15 per cent of the features released in India were Indian and the majority of the rest, comprising foreign films, were American. See Barnouw and Krishnaswamy, *Indian Film* (New York/London: Columbia University Press, 1963).

17 Sumita Chakravarty, *National Identity in Indian Popular Cinema 1947–1987* (Austin: University of Texas, 1993), pp. 33–4.

18 On 7 July 1896, the agents of the Lumiere Brothers held their first film screening of Western films in Bombay, enthralling the city's elite. Indian photographers purchased cameras, started filming shorts and showed them in tents, playgrounds and public halls in Bombay, Calcutta and Madras. The Ephinstone Bioscope Company was started by Jamshedjee

Madan in Calcutta. It incorporated all sectors of the film business. The first cinema house in India, the Madan theatre, was built in Calcutta. The first indigenously produced film was released in 1912. In 1930 the second of India's three major studios—the New Theatres of Calcutta—was established. It had access to sophisticated technology, the power to retain the best talent in the country and determine the films the public should see.

19 See Peiss, *Cheap Amusements,* p. 139. Peiss discusses how the early movie-makers in the United States seemed to be aware of the 'cultural and class divisions marking the terrain of popular amusement' as they sought to address the emerging female audience. She states: 'Linking personal freedom with the culture of consumption and heterosociality . . . these films refashioned the socially appropriate behavior and norms that governed gender relations . . . Visually and thematically these films constructed a notion of modern American womanhood that reaffirmed the cultural style popular among many young American-born working women and . . . . created new aspirations among the foreign born.'

20 Back in Calcutta he worked for Mitsubishi. Just before he was to take a business trip to Japan in 1929, he disappeared. Nobody was ever to hear from him again.

21 On Yom Kippur (Day of Atonement), many families would send their *tirya* to the synagogue where it would be hung. This would enable families to travel by car or public transport to synagogue and then light the oil lamps just before starting the fast. Many families would sleep overnight in the synagogue. Others would walk home, and the *tirya* would be collected by a servant a few days later.

22 By now all the Jewish names were Anglicized. Only when the boys went up to read from the sefer torahs (prayer scrolls) in the synagogues were their Hebrew names used.

23 One such handyman I remember vividly was an odd-job man and electrician called Hazari. He was a Hindu but wore a turban and had a long beard. He rode around town on his old cycle in khaki pants and shirt and canvas shoes. Another legend in the Jewish folklore of Calcutta was Masuda Almana (Masuda the widow), who lived before my time. She carried a kind of oven-hot pita bread on her head to each Jewish home in time for breakfast. Arriving at breakfast time, she would stay on for something to eat and pass on messages and gossip from other homes. She, too, was a regular morning fixture in many middle-class Jewish

homes.

24 This was the case in European homes as well.

25 Raz, now living in the New York area, speaks to me about how he was completely up-to-date on Western musical styles and about the numerous letters he would get from fans all over India.

26 Since Calcutta was the heart of the British empire, the Calcutta Jews were more exposed to Western music and styles than Jews living in Bombay and Cochin. Bombay and Cochin Jews had a greater love for Indian popular music.

27 This club tradition, though less ethnically based, is still strong in Calcutta. However, there are many clubs in the city that are open to all communities and predicated more on class than ethnic or religious lines.

28 The Calcutta Club till today only grants membership to top executives. The rationale here is that these 'burra saabs' can relax at the Club with one another and not have to worry about being seen by their subordinates.

29 As the Jewish community dwindled in the fifties and sixties the club was patronized almost exclusively for gambling purposes. By 1962 the Jewish community consisted of less than a thousand people and was decreasing at the rate of a hundred a year.

30 A few of the elite Jewish women who had married out of the Jewish community, like the Guha sisters, were leaders in Indian women's associations. This points to the fact that when Jewish women wanted to get involved in Indian society and in national struggles and political activity, their involvement was welcomed and they faced no discrimination in holding leadership roles.

31 Sinha, *Calcutta in Urban History,* p. 59.

32 This extended an older tradition where Jewish women, since the nineteenth century, had had access to the andar mahal (inner quarters) of orthodox Indian families. See Tharoor (ed.), *Naari,* p. 10.

33 Here I am referring to Edward Said's definition and discourse on Orientalism where the East is perceived though the Western imaginary. I am not referring to the Orientalist school of thought in colonial India that led to a serious study of ancient Indian texts.

34 Kwame Anthony Appiah discusses extrinsic and intrinsic forms of racism. See 'Racisms' in David Theo Goldberg (ed.), *Anatomy of Racism,* (Minneapolis: University of Minnesota Press, 1990), pp. 3–17.

35 See Jon Stratton, 'The Colour of Jews in Australia: Jews, Race and the White Australia Policy,' in *Journal of Australian Studies,* nos. 50/51, 1996, pp. 51–65.

36 Stratton, in a longer version of the paper quotes a secret letter by T. H. Heyes, the Secretary of the Department of Immigration in 1949, to the Department of External Affairs, stating the government's position thus: 'The Minister holds the view that persons who are not of pure European descent are not suitable as settlers in Australia and it is his desire that those wishing to make homes in this country be not granted the facilities to do so, even though they are predominantly of European extraction and appearance. Persons of Jewish race of Middle Eastern descent are not eligible, under the existing Immigration Policy, for entry to Australia.'

37 Ibid.

38 Stratton points to a case in around 1950 of two brothers and two sisters applying from India, where the brother was granted permission to migrate. After being rejected the sisters arrived in Australia on tourist visas and the immigration officer allowed them to stay in Australia because, as he wrote, 'Miss E. Aaron shows very little trace of color and in my opinion is a quarter caste or less. Her sister appears dark but in my opinion is less than half caste.'

39 The members of a kibbutz all work and in return are supported by the cooperative throughout their lives. An older person with no children entering a kibbutz would by this logic be considered a liability. The kibbutz community would be providing support for someone who had not worked enough years to earn that support. Older people with children could be considered, as their children's labour on the kibbutz would contribute to the support of a parent.

40 'Oseh Haised (Doers of Good Deeds) was founded in the 1880s to provide balm to the broken-hearted and crushed in spirit' (Musleah, *On the Banks of the Ganga*, p. 105). From time to time sums of money were collected to perform the last rites of the indigent. Oseh Haised was primarily founded to ameliorate poverty in the community. It later became a burial society. In 1947 it undertook a humanitarian medical scheme including hospitalization, the supply of nourishment and medicines to the impoverished Jewish sick and aged (p. 325), and a clinic for poor Jews.

41 Clifford, in *Routes,* p. 251.

42 Inderpal Grewal, *Home and Harem: Nation, Gender, Empire and Cultures of Travel* (Durham/London: Duke University Press, 1996), p. 37–53.

43 Salman Rushdie, *Imaginary Homelands* (London: Granta Books, 1991), p. 17.

Flower:
Meeting India at the Midnight Hour

$\mathcal{F}$LOWER (FARHA), THE YOUNGEST CHILD and only daughter of Mary and Elias Abraham, was born in Calcutta in 1930.[1] As the baby of the family and the only girl, she was doted on by her father and was the centre of attention in her home. The character and style of the household was Baghdadi Jewish, overlaid with a strong dose of Victorian discipline and sense of propriety. The Abrahams rented apartments in the north–central area of Calcutta, where many other Jewish families, including many close cousins, resided. My mother vividly recalls the building where she lived as a small girl:

> When I was six years old we lived in an apartment building called Wool House. We had two large rooms, a balcony, and a kitchen. The building was twelve stories high and was on Dharamatalla— a main street—facing the Sacred Heart Church. The balcony, jutting out from our bedroom, was at the height of the church clock. Between us and the church was a very busy street—bustling with shops, vendors, rickshaws, trams, and buses. This building had a lift [elevator], and two doors down from us the first American soda fountain shop opened. I loved the ice-cream and sodas, and my father often took me there as a treat.

From her earliest years Flower grew up in a cosmopolitan environment, and the West had already made an indelible impression on her. She was influenced by the bustle around her and 'tuned in' to the media that provided a window onto the world. Flower recalls:

> From our balcony we could see the large maidan where football and hockey were played. My brothers, friends, and cousins watched matches excitedly from this vantage point. We had an

old-fashioned radio and we listened to the commentary while watching the players in the far distance through a pair of field glasses. The glasses passed from one to another with each person adding their commentary throughout the game.

The Abrahams were surrounded by grandparents, aunts, and cousins who were constantly in and out of each other's homes. Family and community filled their lives. Later, as other members of their family moved further south to the more Anglicized and residential areas of Calcutta, they followed suit. Jewish community life flourished and was probably at its peak in Calcutta during Flower's formative years. With more than 3000 or so Baghdadi Jews living in Calcutta in the 1930s and 1940s, there was an entire set of Jewish institutions, a well-defined community, and lifestyle in place.[2] Middle-class Jewish lives were structured around the family and community with the numerous Jewish festivals, Sabbaths, and weddings as the main events in their social calendars. My mother still recalls with nostalgia the Friday night dinners in her Aunt Matty's home. Mothers, grandmothers and aunts pooled their resources to prepare the meal. Often the cooks of the extended family worked together to prepare the lunch or dinner. Fifteen to twenty family members regularly sat down around a long table to enjoy a Sabbath or festival meal together.

The dishes prepared for Sabbath and festivals were elaborate and involved a great deal of preparation. Every Friday night there was roast chicken and *aloo makallahs, halba* (a fenugreek sauce, Yemenite style) *mahashas* (vegetables stuffed with rice and chicken), a rice *pilao,* and a chicken curry or two. This rather heavy and spicy meal was followed by a selection of fresh fruits. Sabbath prayers and general good cheer lasted late into the night. Saturday mornings were another occasion for family gatherings around a hearty morning meal of steaming *hamim* (chicken stuffed with rice, more chicken, and spices) plus the leftovers from the night before. The *hamim* cooked all Friday night on a slow fire and was eaten as a main meal after the men returned from synagogue. On Saturdays, extended families spent the entire time in each other's company and caught up on news, family and community gossip, and the events of the day. Flower remembers sports—horse racing, boxing, cricket, and hockey—as a topic her family discussed with animation.

Passover and Succoth (Feast of the Tabernacles) were also marked by large family gatherings. It was not uncommon for thirty to forty people to be seated around the seder (Passover) table or in the sukkah. There were so many Jewish homes in the neighbourhoods where my mother grew up that she remembers how, as teenagers, they kept each other posted on the progress of the prayers and tried to speed them up so that they could go out afterwards. My mother recalls: 'In Tottee Lane, where the alleys were so narrow and so quiet, we could hear the services being sung in the Jewish homes around us. We would know where they were in the service. On seder my brother Charles carried the mutka (mud pot) filled with wine symbolizing the ten plagues to be smashed in the street. On returning he chided us, urging us to go faster, letting us know the status of the services in our neighbours' homes.'

In this tight-knit community, in which families lived in adjacent buildings, everybody knew each other's business. They commented on who came and went from each home, and often shouted out messages to one another across the balconies or the compound. My mother remembers Sally Solomon, a neighbour a few years older than she, as the girl next door who regularly practised the piano and was held up as an example to emulate.[3] A smile breaks out on my mother's face as she remembers Sally's father, Mr Luddy, sitting in the compound regaling them with wonderfully funny stories. The community came together more formally during the annual Hanukkah and Purim parties at the Jewish Girls' School. Weddings, bar mitzvahs and brits ranked high among other joyous family occasions that were eagerly awaited and celebrated together. 'I remember,' my mother tells me, 'when I was fourteen, the wedding of my cousin Isaac to Mozelle. This religious and festive affair which took place in the synagogue and the wedding hall, continued for seven days in Aunt Ruby's home. Each night, for one week after the wedding, elaborate dinners were prepared for at least thirty people at a time.' In the spirit of family and community, extended families walked together to and from services on Yom Kippur and the high holidays.

The high holidays fall in late September and early October and coincide with the flamboyant Hindu celebration of Durga Puja in Calcutta. During the Puja (religious festival) which extends over five days, Calcutta is quite transformed. Images of the Goddess Durga, in all her fury and splendour, are installed in colourful puja *pandals* (marquees) across the city. Neighbourhoods compete with each other to mount elaborate *pandals*. Throngs of people, in their new saris and puja outfits, visit the pandals to worship Durga and to admire the artistry of the images. Groups of Jews, however, would walk to and from Kippur services in the midst of these festivities, keeping a distance from the 'idolatry' around them. They tried to ignore the *pandals* and trucks filled with dancing raucous young men taking images of the goddess for immersion in the Hooghly river on the last day of the celebration. My mother remembers her reactions, as a serious and thoughtful girl of nine or ten, to the religious fervour and intensity of other religions:

> Standing silently during the *Amidah* (part of the prayer service), I listened intently to the noises all around us. Drums and cymbals beat loudly from the puja processions, church bells tolled from the Portuguese Catholic Church near the Neveh Shalome (the synagogue where we worshipped), the muezzin called from the big mosque in Zachariah Street, which was in the Muslim neighbourhood of the synagogue. All these insistent, impassioned entreaties to God filled me with awe. I used to wonder why we all had to beseech Him at the same time, and figured He must have trouble heeding all of us at once!

The small Jewish population, though it may have sometimes seemed engulfed and overwhelmed by the religious atmosphere around it, was able to maintain its Jewish identity through its strong sense of community. Its members lived close together, maintained strong family ties, established their own schools, religious institutions, and social spaces. These practices, together with their strict adherence to religious ritual and tradition, gave them a distinct identity and place in Calcutta. According to my mother, 'The ties to Jewishness were tightly bound, making it hard to move out of these confines without facing censure, ridicule, and shame.' Community members lived primarily in Jewish worlds, though they were immersed in non-Jewish surroundings. To maintain their Jewish identity, they felt they had to distance themselves from their surroundings. Marking and observing their difference—and eschewing the 'other'—held them together.

Although tight-knit, the Jewish community was not self-contained. The domestic labour of non-Jews within Jewish homes played an essential role in sustaining the family and helped build and maintain community.[4] Many family meals and celebrations, as well as the maintenance of rituals and customs that are so essential for building community, were made possible by the abundance of local domestic help hired at very low wages. The full-time servants worked on the Sabbath, festivals, and other celebrations to prepare and serve the meals and to clean up. The community inter-preted Jewish law so as to allow the cooks and other domestic help who were non-Jewish to work on the Sabbath, so long as they were not ordered to do so. Servants were often hired on the recommendation of other Jewish families. Trained and trusted help was in high demand.

Many of these full-time and part-time workers were so familiar with Jewish ways and served so many families that they were like extended com-munity—an integral part of everyday life. I have already mentioned the bearded and wiry Hazari, eccentric handyman and electrician, who cycled around furiously to attend to all kinds of repairs in Jewish homes, and who became almost a legend among several generations of Calcutta Jews. On his regular rounds he carried news from one house to another and made wry comments about community members. The servants themselves were a regular topic of conversation.

A middle-class home typically had a cook who ran the kitchen and an ayah who took care of the small children. A 'boy', the cook's assistant, helped him prepare and serve the food, and did a lot of odd jobs and errands. He dusted, polished, and carried goods, food, and 'chits' (notes) from one home to another (telephones were not common in middle-class homes till the late 1940s). There was also the dhobi, bhistiwallah, and jamedar. These part-timers worked for several families and came for a few hours a day or week as required. The bhistiwallah, who carried water in a large goatskin container strapped to his back, had in the past provided water when there was no piped water. Later, despite the facility of run-ning water, he was often needed when power failures cut off the water supply.

Although many of the servants worked their entire lives with one fam-ily, most of the Jews had a colonial relationship with their servants.[5] Too often servants were treated as an anonymous group of people or as chil-dren who needed to be trained and guided in how to behave. Without dis-cipline and guidance servants were expected to relapse back into their 'lazy, irrational ways'. The mistress of the house spent a lot of her time managing the servants' work and the disputes among them. Many Jewish families were quick to blame domestics for missing items, or for cheating on the household accounts. However, it is important to note that servants in India are generally treated in this manner. The servant/employer rela-tionship is inherently hierarchical and patriarchal in its structure. Servants were treated as empty slates: you told them your troubles and they were expected to provide you emotional and material comfort, to listen and to try to make you feel better. As the employer, you never had to recipro- cate by listening to their troubles, although servants might share their trou- bles in the hope of receiving some form of help: a loan or additional wages, or leave from work to take care of the problem.

Even though these were very structured and hierarchical relationships in which the servants knew their place in the family, attachments were often formed between the servants and the employer and other family members. Very often Jewish children spent long hours playing with the ser- vants' children, who quite often would later work for them. These ser- vants enjoyed a special place in the family. I know of Jewish families who have left Calcutta and despite keeping up with very few non-Jews, have stayed in touch with their servants, often sending them money on a regu- lar basis.[6] Many tried to find them alternative or suitable jobs to ensure that the servants would be treated well when they left Calcutta.[7] Sometimes, the servants were the only Indians that the Jews really knew intimately, even though they knew very little about their lives.

Karmalli was among those 'loyal servants' who spent their entire working lives in the service of one family. He was the cook who served my grandmother and mother. Karmalli became our cook when my grand- parents left for Australia. My mother trusted Karmalli implicitly. He always referred to her as 'baba' (young child) rather than Memsaab (Madam). Karmalli, a devout Muslim, tried to run our home on more strict Jewish dietary lines than even my mother herself chose. He often scolded her and threatened to report her to *her* mother! I remember entreating Karmalli to intervene with my mother on our behalf when she had told us children not to do something we wanted to do. Karmalli was like an uncle to us. In addition to being a terrific 'Jewish' cook who cooked the best *aloo makallahs*, he often prepared special treats for us and took us on outings during his time off from work. I remember Karmalli indulgently feeding my elder brother, a slow eater, even when he was a young teenager. When our parents were not there, Karmalli, in his white vest and baggy white pajamas, saw that we ate properly while he told us long stories in Hindustani (the language we spoke at home with the servants) and listened to our escapades with interest. We five children and the other servants all obeyed him when our parents were away from home.

Despite the personal and emotional bonds that sometimes existed between servants and their employers, there is no question in my mind that this relationship was profoundly exploitative.[8] When servants lived in the employer's home or quarters attached to the household, as our servants did, the exploitation increased. Usually, the live-in servants were provided with food, which they cooked for themselves and ate on the premises. Typically, the servants ate from their own utensils while seated on the kitchen floor. They often drank tea together in the kitchen during pre-scribed breaks. Sometimes servants were allowed to take leftover food down to their families. Living on the premises meant that their workdays never ended—they were called upon to provide a service throughout the day and sometimes late into the night. Moreover, a 'good' servant did so uncomplainingly. Thus, servants were not only judged on their work per-formance; their demeanour, attitudes, and personalities had to meet with the approval of their employers as well. Furthermore, domestic servants were expected to live by the rules of the house and always be deferential and loyal. They were meant to be seen but preferably not heard, and were mostly confined to the kitchen, where they could congregate and talk with one another. For loyal and good behaviour a domestic was rewarded at the whim of the employer. The reward could take the form of time off from work, a gift of clothing, food or money, or the goodwill of the family. Thus, these were always paternal and dependent relationships, where power resided with the employers over whose 'beneficence' the servant had little control. The only form of control that servants could exert was to quit their jobs and let others know about the treatment meted out to them in a particular household. The word got around, and some house-holds found it more difficult to keep help.

Like her mother, Flower attended the Jewish Girls' School, which in the 1930s and 1940s was one of the better schools in Calcutta.[9] It was sit-uated in Pollock Street, in the heart of the old Jewish community, in the once Grey area of town. When I asked my mother if the Jewish part of town had a distinct flavour during the time she was growing up, she did not recall it as being distinct from the other parts of town. It seems that by the 1930s this busy residential and commercial area was quite Indian. My mother recalls a co-educational Gujarati-medium school across from Jewish Girls' School. Although the Gujarati children walked in groups to and from school, as did the Jewish children, the two distinct groups of stu-dents never interacted with one another—each was immersed in the world

Above The Abraham family gathers for a bar mitzvah, 1943. Flower is standing in the back row, with a bow n her hair. *Below* A typical Calcutta scene of the forties.

of its own community and did not see or feel the need to venture beyond it. It was common practice for communities to share public spaces without interacting or mixing with one another. Yet there was no hostility—I think there was an acceptance of difference but not the desire to know about each other or to understand the differences that separated them.

The students at Jewish Girls' School were all Jewish, as were most of the staff except for a few Anglo-Indian teachers. The second language was French, and the students learned to read and write enough Hebrew to be proficient at their prayers. Hindi was introduced for the first time in my mother's last year at school. In my mother's generation English was the primary language of school and home. Most students spoke Hindustani, which they picked up from the servants at home and through street interactions. Since the younger generation did not know much Arabic, they spoke to the older people in Hindustani. Although they imbibed Hindustani from the surrounding culture, they never learned to read or write it. In contrast while they learned to read and write Hebrew in school they never understood or spoke it.

The school was the hub of a lot of community activities. The Jewish Women's League, run by wealthy (and some middle-class) women of the community, conducted much of their work at the school. Among the activities of the League were a free milk crèche, a dispensary, a soup kitchen, and free lunches for poorer Jewish children. Most of the social work was geared towards the poorer members of the Jewish community. For the most part, each community in Calcutta provided for their own; however, in times of crisis, the League did contribute to the needs of the broader community.[10]

The school had a kindergarten (for three-year-olds) plus an additional nine grades. In the seventh grade the students had to pass a Junior Cambridge examination, which was administered from and corrected in Cambridge, England. Similarly, in the ninth standard, and to finish high school, they had to pass the Senior Cambridge, the British school-leaving examination. Though this high school education prepared the students for college, most of the girls did not pursue a higher education. They opted for vocational training classes to become teachers, secretaries, nurses, hairdressers, and join other professions that were considered suitable for women in those days. Few middle-class or even wealthy Jewish boys attended college; most joined family businesses or entered a trade. A few elite Jews sent their sons to study in England, and their daughters to attend finishing schools in Europe.

School hours at the Jewish Girls' School were from nine in the morning to three in the afternoon, but schoolwork did not end there. Homework was a regular and daily feature of life, taking at least two hours a day from the first standard. My mother's homework was supervised by her mother, Mary, who drilled Flower in mathematical tables and spelling exercises. Flower was always precocious and loved to read. She excelled in school and proved a gifted student. She ranked among the first ten students in Bengal in her Senior Cambridge examination.[11] This honour was shared with two other Jewish boys from Calcutta. My mother was also very involved in extra-curricular activities, which at the time consisted of choir, acting, and a few sports like netball and badminton. Miss Luddy, the principal of Jewish Girls' School, led an active Girl Guide troop that went on camping trips outside Calcutta. Though Flower longed to be a Girl Guide and go on camping trips with them, her mother did not allow her to do so. 'She did not let me out of her sight for even one night. Exciting accounts of these trips from my friends had to suffice.'

On returning from school, Flower—and most other girls of the community—visited cousins. Flower spent days with both her grandmothers, Simcha and Farha, and also a great deal of time in her Aunt Matty's home. The Joshua home was always bristling with fun because there were eight cousins as well as doting older relatives living there. My mother recalls:

Since I had no ayah I was sent home directly to Aunty Matty's house. I had already eaten the hot lunch that she had sent to school with the servant. Iraqi Jewish food was delivered piping hot in a three-tiered tiffin carrier for her children and me. My grandmother Simcha lived there and always kept goodies for us to eat. She sewed and kept an eye on us while we played. My uncle Simon also lived there. He spent fifteen minutes a day with each of us reading from the torah. The house was full of other cousins. There were great records, and a piano. We played in the courtyard and on the street with all the neighbouring children. The house was bustling with activity. The adult cousins, including my cousin Louise, who was visiting from Shanghai, played mahjong, which we children watched. My brother or older cousins walked me home at about seven in the evening, when I had dinner and got ready for school the next day.

Besides the Joshua household and relatives, Flower visited others in the community. She never went to non-Jewish homes, though she did know a few Anglo-Indians who lived in the neighbourhood.

Sally Solomon, writing about the few Anglo-Indian neighbours with whom she played as a child, underscores the unstated distance-maintenance that was observed between Jews and others. 'I cannot remember going upstairs to my neighbours, the Marleys', or the Marleys being invited to dinner. It seemed to be understood on both sides, that while we would always be good friends, family affairs would remain private.' Solomon also describes her first visit to the home of an Indian friend, when she was eighteen and in college in Calcutta. She describes how her father reluctantly granted her permission, perceptively noting the nervousness of both families with that encounter:

> Daddy was watching my growing friendship, through table tennis, with a young Indian boy, my doubles partner in several championships. His family was well-known in our community so I did not think there would be any hitch in asking, one day, 'Daddy can I go to Anil's house and listen to some music?' Daddy's first reaction was not positive. His silence said it all. I began to feel a growing resentment at his unspoken disapproval.

When Sally arrived at Anil's home, his two maiden aunts delicately questioned her about her background. She looks back on their discomfort: 'I must have been as much a threat to this aristocratic Bengali family as their son and heir was to my own. While the music played I sat comfortably in this Western style environment, knowing more surely that my friendship with Anil would be nothing more than platonic.'[12]

These very circumscribed interactions with 'friends' from other communities point to how Jews distrusted friendships beyond the circle of the community. When members from different communities mixed, their interactions were limited to the playground or other such public spaces. While several Jewish boys did have Anglo-Indian girlfriends, they would only bring them home if there was a party. It might have been all right to go out with Anglo-Indian girls, but it was not acceptable for Jews to marry outside the community. An invisible but well-defined line was drawn between public interactions and the intimacy of the home, which was reserved for members of the same community. The separation between

Jews and others was reciprocal; most communities feared that relationships and friendships could eventually lead to an unwanted intermarriage.

The streets of central Calcutta served as playgrounds where children spun tops, played gulli danda (ball and stick), kick-the-can, or marbles, climbed trees, cycled, skated, and flew kites from the rooftops. My mother recalls how all the kids in the neighbourhood, including the servants' children, joined in. Indoor games among the Jews included mahjong, recently introduced from Shanghai. Other common games were cards, touli and Monopoly. Western movies were very popular, and Jewish youngsters often attended the cinema in large groups. Flower and her cousins, the Joshuas, had a fixed weekly reservation for the entire year at the Metro cinema, which was not far from their home. This was such a weekly ritual that a friend of Flower's often quipped that when her brother Charles died, instead of lighting a memorial light for him, they would reserve Charles a seat in the Metro cinema. Flower vividly recalls the Metro and its meaning for them:

> The Metro was the most modern of the cinemas till the Lighthouse was built in the early 1940s. The Metro had lush red velvet carpeting and upholstery. The heavy burgundy-lined draperies with gold fringes and heavy tassels were the height of elegance for us. The way in which the curtains fell and moved to reveal the silver screen was almost magical. Going to the movies was an event that lasted the entire week. We planned it a week ahead, bought our tickets, met our friends, and dressed in our good clothes for the occasion. Ice-cream, masala popcorn, and chips were treats at the interval, and we always came home to try and play the music on the piano without the scores. When we perfected the music, we would then dance to it—so the movies extended beyond the movies. We would often sketch the clothes the stars wore so that the local durzee could sew it for us. This often entailed going twice to the same movie to make sure we got the score and the styles down right!

The youngsters in the Jewish community saw themselves as decidedly modern. The movies—and their interactions with the entire spectacle of cinema and cinema-going—facilitated the development of their individual and community imaginings.

In addition to the movies they kept up with music and the stars. My mother recalls: 'I was a fan of Frank Sinatra as an eleven year-old bobby soxer—though my older cousins were all old faithfuls of Bing Crosby. We read the silver screen magazines, cut out pictures of film stars, and had pin-ups in our bedrooms.' Later my mother and her cousins enjoyed the weekly teen parties, where they danced to Western-style music on windup gramophones in various neighbourhood homes. A few Anglo-Indian girls, friends of some of the boys, sometimes joined the party. Jiving, jitterbugging, and other ballroom dances were very popular. They learned the dance steps from one another till they became adept at them. The Judean Club held dances and socials, but only those over eighteen could attend because gambling and drinking were allowed on the premises. Flower's generation of middle-class Jews, even more so than their parents' generation, kept up with cultural influences from America and England. So, before the direct impact of the West on their lives during World War II, it was the cinema and the music associated with it that enabled them to construct what Arjun Appadurai has called 'imagined selves and imagined worlds'.[13] The media and cinema provided resources to experiment with self-making and gave them the tools to infuse their lives with the glamour of filmstars and Hollywood. As consumers of a great deal of Western films and media, my mother's generation looked to the West as their social and cultural reference point. They aspired to be Western and it seemed within their reach. Though they were, for the most part, less religiously observant than their parents and grandparents, strong residuals of Jewishness also determined their worldviews. However, their Middle Eastern practice of Judaism was significantly overlaid with Western culture that could not be separated from who they were and sought to be.

The outbreak of World War II in the year 1939 deeply affected Jewish community life and the Calcutta in which it grew and flourished. Flower was nine when the war broke out and even at that young age she was aware of and curious about the foreign presence in the city.

> I suddenly saw a new Calcutta. There was an influx of foreign, uniformed men in the streets. They rode around in jeeps and trucks and I clearly remember seeing airplanes for the first time. The planes landed on the Red Road—a strip of concrete beyond the maidan. To and from school we passed their 'billets' and wondered where these men came from and why they were here. Later some Jewish soldiers came into our homes and we slowly became more familiar with them. We were amazed that they were

Jewish like us, though they looked and behaved so differently.

At an early age she realized that there were other kinds of Jews in the world and though they were very different from her, she tried to make a place for them in her small world.

Among the students and in the community, the War took centre stage and was followed closely by all. Flower remembers detailed coverage of war events in school drawn from the English newspapers and from Radio Ceylon (also in English). Flower, along with other girls, took turns writing up headline news on a blackboard at the entrance of the school because not all the girls received newspapers at home. The events were discussed and analysed by the teachers and students in their current events class. At first the War was still far away in Europe and had little bearing on India. My mother recalls, however, that the distant events became part of her world through the media: 'In our world history classes we had maps posted on the bulletin boards and we plotted the advances of the various armies. In this way we could literally see Germany gobbling up most of Europe. Images of the War from the news, screened before the feature film, made the headline news come to life for us.'

My mother tells me that it was not till 1940-41 that the Jews of Calcutta received news of what was happening to Jews in Europe. This aspect of the War hit them directly when the first group of Jewish refugees from Europe arrived in Calcutta. About thirty Polish Jews had escaped over Asia to Japan and from there were making their way to Palestine. They had docked in Calcutta and could not proceed on their journey because the oceans were mined. These refugees temporarily became part of the community. This gave Calcutta Jews some firsthand accounts of what was happening to Jews in Europe. Flower vividly recalls one of the young men, who became a family friend over the years:

> Some of these men lived in my neighbourhood. I remember Bolek Rembaum, a dashingly handsome young man who was our basketball and hockey coach. Bolek at first could not speak English but he soon became fluent and gave us firsthand, troubling accounts of the Warsaw ghetto—it was the first time I had ever heard about the plight of the Jews there. Bolek stayed on in Calcutta and married one of the girls next door who was about ten years older than me. He became part of the Calcutta Jewish community. Starting with a small import/export business in a

rented room where he traded in women's dresses and cosmetics he rose to become a very successful businessman. He died in Calcutta in the eighties.

Through the handful of European Jews like Bolek who sought refuge in Calcutta as Nazism raged in Europe, many Calcutta Jews came to know Jews who were different from themselves and to learn about a Jewish world beyond that of their diaspora community.

The War inched ever closer to Calcutta. In December 1941 the Japanese invaded Pearl Harbor and marched through Southeast Asia into Burma on the Bengal border. My mother remembers the Burmese refugees who also sought refuge in Calcutta in 1943: 'As the war progressed and came nearer we saw the refugees from Burma trek their way into India. This included members of the Jewish community of Rangoon who told us of their harrowing treks through the jungle where some lost their lives.' A few air raids on Calcutta led to the evacuation of many women and children from the city. Continued air raids saw entire families evacuate to Darjeeling, Madhupur, Bombay, or Delhi. Because Flower's mother did not want to leave Calcutta, she decided to send Flower, along with a handful of other Jewish girls, to a boarding school till the threat subsided. Thus a Christian, co-educational school in Nagpur, suddenly had three Jewish girls on its rolls. In 1943 Flower felt herself as if airlifted from a totally Jewish world to a totally Christian, Anglo-Indian one. It was a transformative year for her. It was her first experience of life beyond the confines of the Calcutta Jewish community.

Bishop Cotton, Nagpur, is a missionary school in central India. There Flower came into direct contact with the New Testament scriptures, church, and the choir. She also made many Christian friends. This world and the lifestyle of her friends and fellow students were very different from her own. The differences she encountered ran the gamut from eating different types of food, including non-kosher foods, though her mother had requested her to eat only vegetarian food, to singing in the school church choir. She was for the first time exposed to people with very different social norms. In particular, the social and sexual mores for the girls and boys were a lot more liberal than those of the Jewish community. This firsthand experience of another way of life broadened her outlook tremendously. After Flower had been away for a year, her mother insisted that, because Calcutta was safer by now, her daughter must return to the Jewish

Girls' School for her last two years of school. Flower kept in touch with her non-Jewish friends, despite her mother's disapproval. Thus, the exposure to Anglo-India and a non-Jewish world did not end when she came back to the Jewish Girls' School. It remained a point of contention between her and her mother, who forever regretted her decision to send Flower away. While Flower had met Anglo-India and a world beyond her community, she had not as yet encountered the 'Indian' within India.

By the time Flower returned to Calcutta from Nagpur, there were British and American troops stationed in and around Calcutta because the city was the base of the Southeast Asia command under Lord Mountbatten. The troops included many American and British Jews. They were invited to Calcutta Jewish homes and became involved in the community's religious and social life. Sally Solomon describes the impact of the soldiers on the community: 'The first change that struck me on my return to Calcutta after a year, was to see the city filling up with servicemen from overseas; large areas were requisitioned for camps and bases, and khaki-clad men and women became a common sight. The uniformed men dotted in the streets were soon in and out of our homes, dating the girls, many of whom broke off existing alliances to make new ones with soldiers, sailors and airmen who showered them with gifts and promises. There was an excitement in the air, filled with guilt, and fear . . .' Solomon then describes her father's response to the servicemen's dating Jewish girls: 'Even though he joked, deep down was the gnawing fear of his daughters being lured away to foreign lands, perhaps by non-Jews, and with little hope of returning. But for us, the younger generation, the War had magically opened doors which we thought were closed forever.'[14]

Flower was an active and founding member of the Young People's Congregation along with Ezekiel Musleah. This Jewish youth group burgeoned under the principal tutelage of David J. Seligson, an American army chaplain. Seligson, who in civilian life was the spiritual leader of the Central Synagogue in New York City, and Bloch, a British Jewish chaplain, were both posted in Calcutta to minister to the troops. Flower became particularly attracted by Jewish practices and ideas that Seligson and Bloch introduced to her. She heard that women could play a more active role in services and liked the idea of girls and boys sitting together rather than separately, as had been the custom. With the guidance of Seligson, the Congregation experimented with these new ideas. They conducted Sabbath services after the regular services at the Beth-el synagogue incorporating some of these innovations. The services attracted young people partly because they were held in English and Hebrew. A sermon in English was introduced each week and conducted by one of the young members of the congregation on a topic relevant to the reading of the week. Both Ezekiel Musleah and my mother led some of these services. While the Calcutta Jews all knew how to read Hebrew, they did not understand the Hebrew prayer, so the English interventions were very welcome. This was the first time the community had encountered such non-traditional practices. While the community was very traditional and vigorously safeguarded its Jewish identity and practices, its members did not feel at all threatened by changes that came from the Jewish community outside India and thus did not oppose these innovations. Living in India for so many years, they were open to adaptations and probably saw them as modern ways to keep their youth interested in and attracted to Judaism. In this process Flower was introduced to new Jewish norms and was encouraged, she says, 'to search for less traditional norms in every sphere of life.'

My mother speaks about a memorable Yom Kippur service that was organized by Chaplain Seligson towards the end of the War. It was held in the skating rink of Monsoon Square Gardens. She says that five thousand British and American servicemen were flown into Calcutta from all over the Southeast Asia command, some over the Hump (Tibet), to attend the service. These Jews of various nationalities and races came through difficult terrain to pray together on this auspicious day. Sitting in their midst, she felt for the first time that she was part of a larger Jewish world. Her imagined community of Jews had expanded beyond the Baghdadi diaspora of her mother and grandmothers to include all Jews.

My mother was deeply moved by momentous happenings outside the Jewish community. At thirteen she witnessed the Bengal Famine of 1943, which brought great misery and hardship to the poor throughout Bengal. She says that it was her first close-up glimpse of the mass suffering and starvation of people who lived around her. Images of the famine were on the newsreels, and accounts of the suffering were broadcast on the radio. She witnessed long lines of starving people waiting for a handful of rice. Many of the domestic servants flocked back to their villages. Though the famine did not affect the middle classes of Calcutta directly, it did leave a lasting impression on Flower. She became acutely aware of the suffering caused by political machinations. She remembers that hardly was the famine over when refugees poured into Bengal from Burma after the Japanese attack. While a handful of refugees were from the Jewish community and were taken care of, there were thousands of others who had no homes and were living on the streets. One wave of misery seemed to follow the next in those tumultuous times. There were numerous outbreaks of disease that hit the city—lice, scabies and typhoid among them.

Flower was barely fifteen when the Hindu–Muslim riots broke out as the bloody prelude to Partition. Curfews were imposed to contain the riots, as fear and death stalked the streets. The domestic servants working for Jewish families once again fled to their villages for safety, while the Jews stood by and watched the carnage. Hindus and Muslims warned their Jewish neighbours not to take sides but to keep out of the fray. Thus, though in the midst of these events, they were removed and watched as if from a distance. According to my mother they tried as best they could to continue with their lives, all the while feeling that these battles swirling around them were being fought by others and were outside their sphere of influence and control. She recalls her brother's experience when he and a Jewish friend (who was in the British army and thus had access to an Army jeep) were driving through communal riots along with their dhobi. The dhobi, insecure about getting through the riot-torn city unscathed, could not deliver their clothes to their home as was the usual custom. So they were on their way to the ghat (the place on the riverbank where washing was done) to fetch their clothes. On the way they passed a mob attacking a pregnant woman. When they stopped to try and help her, the mob knew immediately that they were not Hindu, Muslim or British and thus warned them not to interfere. Should they take sides the mob would be forced to turn on them, too. The young Jewish men felt guilty about leaving this gruesome scene without helping the distressed woman. The mob waited for the jeep to go on its way and then resumed their ferocious attack.

The episode exemplifies a double distancing—the two young men out to get their clothes in a riot-torn city, and the locals' demand that the Jews remain uninvolved in their battles—and suggests that Jewish political dis-engagement was to some extent directly related to how the Jews were per-ceived in India. It also underscores the almost pathological compartmen-talization of differences, in which an angry and ferocious mob would stop their attack to let those 'different' from them pass and then resume their business. It is an incident in which the local people acknowledged and respected the Jews, but as outsiders. The locals did not see them as part of their world. As long as the Jews stayed out of local politics and battles, they would not be hurt in any way and could continue with their lives.

In a less sombre story about lack of Jewish engagement in politics of the time, Flower recalls having to stay home Saturday after Saturday in 1946 as regular curfews were imposed to contain the pre-Partition riots and incidents of communal violence. Flower and her friends decided to 'beat the system' by organizing their Saturday night parties as 'curfew parties'. These parties differed from the regular Saturday night flings. They required the guests to dance and jive all night till the curfew ended, since the boys and girls could neither sleep over (for reasons of social prohibition as well as lack of space) nor leave during curfew hours. As they jitterbugged to Benny Goodman, Artie Shaw, and Glenn Miller inside the safety of their homes, outside on the streets fear and foreboding loomed menacingly. These incidents serve as metaphors for the ambiguous political identity of the Calcutta Jews who, neither British nor Indian, lived between the two worlds, never a part of either.

Flower had tasted freedom in Nagpur for a year when she left the tight confines of Jewish life in Calcutta. She was anxious to get away from what she perceived as 'a claustrophobic Jewish community environment', and she set her heart on attending college outside Calcutta to experience a larger world. Her mother insisted that, if she was to leave Calcutta at all, it would have to be to Lady Irwin College—a home science college in Delhi—because the principal and one of the founders, Hannah Sen, was a Jewish woman.[15] Moreover, ever watchful and cautious, Mary felt somewhat reassured that three other girls from the community had been there and had returned home unscathed and still Jewish. Thus, though Flower had no interest whatsoever in home science (and was still in the process of figuring out what she wanted to study), she accepted her mother's terms. She seized this opportunity to be away from home for a while.

Flower did not arrive at Lady Irwin on the opening day of college because she had to attend the wedding of her brother, Eric. Instead of joining the Calcutta party of girls on the journey to Delhi, she was to follow two weeks later on her own. During those weeks Direct Action Day took place, accompanied by strikes and curfews. Rail transport was cancelled, except for military trains, and there was no way to get to Delhi, which was thousands of miles away. So Flower was smuggled aboard a military train dressed in WAC (Women's Army Corp) uniform, by her brother's friend who was in the British army and was on his way to Simla via Delhi to be demobilized. My mother remembers: 'I wore a knee-length khaki cotton skirt with a fitted jacket that had brass buttons and lapels, and on my head was a jaunty service cap. I thought I looked quite trendy. My brother's friend teased me right through the trip but thought I looked the part!'

Lady Irwin College, founded in 1932, was a project of the All India Women's Conference (AIWC), the principal all-India women's organiza-tion. Started in 1927, it was concerned from the outset with the issue of women's education and educational reform. Its charter stated its desire to develop an education that would be suitable for Indian women to best per-form their roles in the home. By 1928 it began to collect funds to open Lady Irwin College, which was to be a domestic science college in Delhi. While advocating home science for Indian women, AIWC had a separate educational strategy for poor women, promoting vocational education so that they would better be able to support themselves.[16] By the late 1930s AIWC was deeply involved in the nationalist cause.[17] Thus, Lady Irwin College became a focal point for Congress activities. Famous Congress women leaders such as Rajkumari Amrit Kaur, Vijaylakshmi Pandit, and Sarojini Naidu were active in determining the direction and political ori-entation of the college and figured prominently in college activities and events.

The active involvement of women in the nationalist struggle gave women 'a new dignity in public life, a new confidence . . . and made them . . . active subjects or agents of reform.'[18] In keeping with Congress sen-timents and the ideology of the Indian women's movement, women were proclaimed the 'mothers of the nation'. The nation was seen as the natu-ral extension of the family, and women, who were the moral guardians and bearers of tradition in the home would now carry forth this noble tradi-tion in the larger national home, the nation. Thus the establishment of a home science college for women was a direct application of this national-ist ideology, with its iconography of the home and domestic space. The new women of India that this college sought to mould were—through their selfless performance of domestic duties and by instilling the right values in their children—to be the builders of a new and vigorous India. During Flower's first few weeks at college in September 1946, she saw Mahatma Gandhi, Jawaharlal Nehru, Vallabhai Patel, and other major Congress per-sonalities on campus. Flower was very interested in politics and says that she was 'dumbfounded to realize that all these great leaders were part of the regular college atmosphere.' They were inspirational, and she became committed to the national struggle.

Women from all over India, of different faiths, plus a few students from Africa and Ceylon, attended Lady Irwin. Most students were Hindu, Sikh, or Muslim, but there were also a few Indian Christians and Jewish girls at the college. The founders of the college were wedded to Congress ideals and sought to create a 'composite nationality' from the diverse cultures of India, stressing the values and importance of cultural assimilation and social intermingling between different religions, creeds, and classes.[19] Accordingly, the students all lived together in dormitories in the spirit of national unity. However, the students were encouraged and expected to publicly maintain their own traditions and heritage. Each morning the assembly began with a prayer service of a different religious denomination. When her turn came, Flower conducted assemblies in Hebrew and shared Jewish traditions with her fellow students. The college officially celebrated all the religious festivals of the different communities represented at the college. Through her participation in all religious services Flower learned a reverence for all religions that stayed with her all her life. She 'remembers waking up at four o'clock on a cold winter morning to join the Sikh girls in celebrating Guru Nanak's birthday. We all sang hymns and they distributed hot prasad (sanctified food offerings) to all the students. Before I came to Delhi other religions were completely unknown to me.'

While Flower knew that her mother would disapprove of her involvement and participation in the prayers and rituals of different religions, she found this aspect of college exhilarating. Through her involvement in such college activities as prayer ceremonies, marches, singing of nationalist songs, and through a better understanding of Congress ideals of 'unity in diversity' she realized for the very first time that 'being Indian could encompass being Jewish'. For the very first time she saw a way to proclaim her Indianness and her Jewishness and not have these two identities conflict with one another. It was a revelation to her and directly contradicted what she had learned in the Jewish community, where Indianness was seen as a threat to Jewish identity.

In addition to coming into direct contact with nationalist politics at Lady Irwin, Flower had her first encounters with Indians as close friends. To fit in with the other students at the college, Flower often wore salwar kameez (a north Indian women's outfit), which was what the majority of

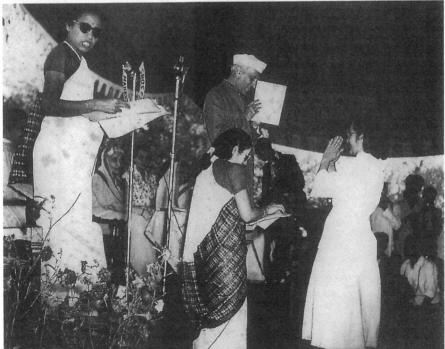

Above Flower was President of the Lady Irwin College students' union, 1948-49; she is seated third from left in the front row. *Below* Receiving her graduation diploma from Jawaharlal Nehru.

Flower with Pamela Mountbatten at Lady Irwin College, 1947-48.

the students wore. She learned a more formal Hindi, learned to sing Hindi national songs, ate Indian food with her fingers, listened to popular Hindi music, and tried to familiarize herself with Indian culture, which was all very new to her. 'At home in Calcutta we had some Indian food but we never ate a completely Indian meal. I had never eaten on a thali (platter) before. In college we only ate Indian food off thalis. There were many dishes I had never eaten before like *biryani, bhaturas, mattar paneer, and gaajar halwa*. I also learned to make these dishes.' Flower remembers taking Frank Sinatra records to college. Her friends introduced her to popular Indian singers whom they enjoyed. Many came from Westernized Indian families and were familiar with the songs of Frank Sinatra and other Western singers.

Flower played the piano and led the college's Christian choir. There were choirs for each of the denominations, but since there were so few Jewish students there was no Jewish choir. As part of the Christian choir she regularly attended the prayer meetings and services on campus and went to Birla House to sing the ecumenist Gandhi's favourite Christian hymn, 'Lead Kindly Light' at his prayer meetings.[20] She would stay up till late at night finding out about the religious beliefs and practices of her classmates. Like the other students, she kept abreast of political events— the independence movement had captured their imaginations.

On weekends and holidays Flower was often invited to the homes of students who lived in the Punjab and in the vicinity of Delhi, and still recalls their warm hospitality. The story I remember best is about the time her friend's parents came to the station through which the girls were passing in the middle of the night to hand them piping hot food in a tiffin carrier. The girls were from broad-minded Indian homes, which allowed them to live away from home and attend a boarding college. Their families welcomed Flower. This was the first time she really travelled in India as an Indian and got a taste of what India was all about.

> I travelled by third-class train with other students from the college and would wear salwar kameez, eat foods sold at the stations en route, and drink tea in mutkas (clay cups). We went to visit the homes of other Indian students, while before I had only been with other Jews. Jews usually travelled in self-contained groups, taking food and provisions along. I remember travelling to Delhi with my mother, two grandmothers, an aunt, and various cousins

at the age of twelve. We had a compartment to ourselves and the servant came along with us. We could not buy food along the way except for a few Indian sweets with which we were familiar, because it would not have been kosher. My fellow students introduced me to new kinds of food specialities that were picked up at stations along the route from Calcutta to Delhi.

When Flower stepped outside her own world into another that was alien to her, she became a part of that other world, even though it was for a brief period of three years.

Flower was on her summer vacation in Calcutta when she heard Jawaharlal Nehru make his famous speech, listening to the radio spellbound as he spoke, ushering in the new nation and imploring India to take its rightful moral place in the family of nations:

At the stroke of the midnight hour, when the world sleeps, India will awake to life and freedom. A moment comes, which comes rarely in history, when we step out from the old to the new, when an age ends and when the soul of a nation, long suppressed, finds utterance. It is fitting at this moment that we take the pledge of dedication to the service of India and her people and to the still larger cause of humanity.

That night Flower and her cousins joined in the festivities and celebrated India's independence by lighting firecrackers and riding a *ghora-garry* (horse carriage) through the city. When she returned to Lady Irwin in September, the refugees from Punjab had started pouring into Delhi by train, foot, and bullock cart. Makeshift shelters for the refugees had been constructed very close to Lady Irwin and the College became a depot for food and medicine, which the college students would regularly distribute among the refugees.

As a sequel to Partition, Hindu-Muslim riots broke out on Delhi streets. Lady Irwin College was in a Sikh and Hindu neighbourhood. A number of Muslim students, including a number of scholarship students, wards of the Nizam of Hyderabad, were living in the dormitories. The Sikh mob got wind of this and surrounded the college, demanding that the Muslims be handed over to them. They threatened to set the college on fire unless the girls were released. Hannah Sen, the principal, stepped in and took charge of this potentially dangerous situation. She smuggled the students into an underground room and announced to the mob that the

Above left Metro Cinema, a favourite with Flower. *Above right* Flower was comfortable wearing Indian clothes such as the salwar kameez for women, as in this photograph taken in college. *Below* Board members, staff and boarders at the Jewish Girls' School hostel, 1961.

girls had already returned to Hyderabad. Meanwhile, the girls were kept hidden for three weeks in an underground room in the college before they could be smuggled safely out of Delhi. In this volatile environment Flower and the other students were instructed on how to defend themselves. They learned how to do a lathi charge (wielding a stick as a weapon of self-defence), and sulfuric acid, chili powder, and empty bottles were kept ready on the roof to be hurled down by the students should a mob attack the college.

The tide of refugees from both India and Pakistan kept swelling. Starving people trekked with their families between the two newly constructed nations in the hope of reaching safety on the other side. Lady Irwin College served as the focal point for 'Operation Chapati'. For one long night the college became a base for making chapatis by the thousands. Indian air force planes picked up the chapatis from the college and flew between the border and Delhi. The airlifted bundles were dropped to the refugees to stem starvation and fatigue. The plight of the refugees came home to Flower when many of the students at Lady Irwin from the Punjab returned to college as refugees. Flower had visited some of their homes in the Punjab (now part of West Pakistan) a year earlier. The families of these girls had lost all their possessions and property, and they had to build their lives anew. In those brief few months two new nations were birthed in bloodshed. In that violent birthing thousands died and many lives were shattered and irrevocably changed. Partition and its horrors have left a deep impression on my mother and most of her generation.

In her last year of college in 1948 India become a republic. Flower was there for that memorable event in January—a historic moment filled with pomp and pageantry. A few months earlier, she had very proudly received her diploma from Lord Mountbatten, the last Viceroy of India who had come with the express purpose of handing over the reins of government. In 1949 she received her graduating diploma from Pandit Nehru. To her he was a hero, as he was to most of the nation and to many throughout the world. For that occasion she wore a white Western-style suit made of sharkskin fabric with the top tailored to resemble Nehru's achkan (high-collared men's jacket).

These few years after independence were times of heady nationalism and great idealism for many in India who saw the future filled with promise. Flower was among those caught up in the euphoria of independence.

She and other students would walk past Nehru's home in Teen Murti Lane late at night to catch a glimpse of him sitting at his desk near the window, doing the work of the nation. 'From the street we would see only a silhouette of him bent over his desk, but it gave us a great uplifting feeling—we felt our country was safe in his hands.' While some like Flower felt safe in the new India, Partition left fear, agony, and uncertainty among many, and permanent scars on the nation.[21]

Communal tensions continued to simmer and erupted, barely five months after independence, over the status of Kashmir. The Mahatma, who had categorically rejected an independence based on the partition of India, was further repulsed at the anguish and bloodshed unleashed in the battle over Kashmir's status.[22] On 12 January Gandhi announced his decision to fast as a protest against the persecution of Muslims in India's capital and to restore 'heart friendship' among Indians of every region. He said: 'Let my fast quicken conscience, not deaden it. Just contemplate the rot that has set in beloved India.'[23] During January Gandhiji fasted and held regular prayer meetings at Birla House to promote national unity. Flower and the college choir sang at these meetings as the nation entered its first new year in 1948, but there were many others, especially Hindu fundamentalists, who did not support Gandhi and his belief in Hindu-Muslim reconciliation.

On 30 January my mother did not attend the prayer service because she had decided to see a BBC docudrama. That day, as Gandhi walked to the platform for the prayer meeting at the garden of Birla House, he was shot by Nathuram V. Godse, a member of the Rashtriya Swayamsevak Sangh (RSS). She recalls:

> We had barely sat down when the film was stopped and we heard the dreadful news. We ran to the gate and found that the girls who had gone to the meeting had come back shaken and crying, relating to us what they had witnessed. About this time the radio announced that he had died. First they had said he had been wounded. Gandhi had been killed by a Hindu extremist who believed he was too pro-Muslim. Gandhiji died with the name of God on his lips after just having come out of a fast to coerce his followers to transfer a larger share of the assets of an undivided India to Pakistan.

Nehru, in his nationwide broadcast that evening announced, 'The light has gone out of our lives and there is darkness everywhere.[24] Flower was deeply shaken by the assassination of the Mahatma, as was the rest of the nation and the world. Bhajans (devotional songs) and other hymns were sung for him around the clock. Flower sang with the college choir and mourned him through the mourning period.

Flower's brief but formative encounter with Indian nationalism made her feel, for the first time, that she was both an Indian and a Jew. India and Indians, which her parents had always presented to her as 'foreign', no longer seemed so. It was a place, a people, and a struggle with which she could now identify. She felt that, when she identified with India, she was accepted and not treated as an outsider. For example, at Lady Irwin, Flower was elected the president of the student's union in her final year (1948-49) at a time when nationalist sentiments ran high. She took an active part in college affairs that were closely tied to Indian national politics. Her experience suggests that when Jews wanted to identify themselves as Indians, there was no resistance to their doing so, and their participation was welcomed.[25]

Flower, on her return to Calcutta from college, was planning to study nutrition at Columbia University, New York. Her friend, Ezekiel Musleah, who had left Calcutta to study at the Union Theological Seminary in New York, encouraged her to take up postgraduate studies at Columbia. However, her plans changed rather abruptly as she was swept off her feet by David Silliman, also from the Calcutta community. They first met at the Judean Club after he had come back from working in England, and they worked briefly on co-ordinating the varied activities of Jewish organizations in Calcutta. David was a direct descendant of Shalome Cohen, a consummate businessman, entrepreneur, and founding member of the community. The Cohen family dominated the economic and spiritual life of the community for two generations and continued to have a significant influence until the community dispersed.

My father never passed up an opportunity to remind us of his 'noble' lineage. I grew up admiring the black-and-white, delicately drawn, aristocratic portrait of Shalome Cohen that is featured in the standard accounts of Calcutta Jewry. Most histories of the Calcutta Jewish community recount the colourful life of Shalome Cohen, the first Arabic-speaking Jew to settle in Calcutta. He was born in Aleppo, Syria, in 1762. In 1790, this ambitious young adventurer made an exploratory business journey to Surat and Bombay. After his initial visit he decided to undertake another voyage to India in 1792. This time he came with the intention of settling in this land so rich in business opportunities. After several trips back and forth between Syria and Calcutta he decided to settle in Calcutta which, at the turn of the eighteenth century, was a centre for trade and the commercial heart of British India.

Shalome was a jeweller by profession who traded in diamonds, silks, indigo, and Dacca cloth. As his businesses flourished, he brought in other Jews from Aleppo and Cochin to assist him in his commercial ventures. Family members were integral to his business: his younger brother, Abraham, was designated his commercial envoy to Bombay, and other relatives were dispatched regularly to other trading centres like Muscat and Basra as his representatives. Shalome was appointed the court jeweller to the Nawab of Lucknow in 1816. This was a high honour, for the Nawab was among the wealthiest princes in the region. Shalome's knowledge of gems was rewarded most handsomely. The Nawab invested him with the distinguished and royal 'Robe of Honour'. Shalome was also granted the unique distinction of riding with the Nawab on his elephant.[26] Calcutta folklore has it that he valued the Kohinoor diamond for Maharaja Ranjit Singh.[27] Shalome established connections with other princes in the region, the British viceroy, and foreign consuls and dignitaries. His diary records Jewish, Muslim, and Christian auspicious dates, demonstrating his versatility and familiarity with different cultural traditions.[28]

David, always a rebel, on finishing high school, joined a merchant navy ship as a cabin boy to get away and avoid joining the family business. He made several trips abroad and eventually worked in London for about fourteen months with the Jewish Agency before the establishment of the state of Israel. Soon after David returned to India in 1949 his father died unexpectedly. As the eldest son, David read the kaddish for his father. It was during this time, when he was somewhat involved with the community, that he met Flower, although they moved in very different circles. Flower found him 'charming, outgoing, and a lot of fun'. Two years later they married. For their wedding in April, 1951, they had a small gathering at the synagogue, followed by a reception at Flower's aunt's large home, which family and friends attended. David's uncle threw a large cocktail party following the reception for many of their European and Indian business associates, after which the couple went to Europe for a six-month honeymoon. Their extravagant honeymoon was highly unusual—at most,

Jewish couples like them would go to Darjeeling or to the seaside at Gopalpur for a week or two. David, however, wanted to show his bride the world, and insisted on making this voyage by P&O Steamship Company (a British line) from Bombay to Southampton. In England they bought a car and motored through Scotland and Europe. Flower remembers:

> The honeymoon was a very exciting time in my life. However, visiting Europe in 1951 was very disturbing. I saw destroyed buildings all over Italy, and I saw parts of Essen, Bremen, and Cologne still in ruins. I remember passing a road sign with an arrow pointing to Auschwitz. The rest of the day was passed in stunned silence. In England there was still food rationing and clothing was on points. People were struggling to rebuild their homes and their lives. We were young and still enjoyed this memorable visit.

After the honeymoon David returned to the foreign exchange business that had belonged to his family for three generations. The firm, D. A. Silliman and Co., was almost a hundred years old. Flower and David decided to stay on in India even though many Jewish people were moving out of the country:

> David had a family business to run and so we felt economically secure. He would learn the business from his uncle who had brought him up. We started our life very modestly in a small apartment. We had blown away the money he had made on the stock exchange on our honeymoon, so with a modest inheritance we started life with very little. We did have a Morris Minor that we brought back from London. After four years in three different apartments and two children we finally found the home we have till today.

They were quite confident in their decision to remain in Calcutta. My father had lived in England for a while and was not enamoured of it. He felt he could be someone in Calcutta, while the future seemed a lot more uncertain in England. My mother felt that she could be part of the new India that was being created and looked forward expectantly to her future.

Flower's marriage to David brought great changes in her life. She travelled from one social class to another and moved from the Jewish community to a much wider and more cosmopolitan world. Her parents did not approve of her marriage partner or her new lifestyle, which was so far

Flower as a bride, 1951.

Flower and David cutting their wedding cake, 1951.

removed from their world and religious orientation. The Sillimans moved not only in Indian but also in international circles in Calcutta because many of David's clients were foreigners working for foreign banks. Flower reinvented herself as a 'memsaab' as she crossed these boundaries. Looking back at this phase of her life, she says: 'It was a difficult transition for me. Growing up, I attended and enjoyed informal parties where we jived and danced to Big Bands on gramophone records. Now, in formal evening wear, I had to stand around, smile, and pretend to be someone else. I had to learn to drink whisky and enjoy it, and was expected to make small talk with very boring people whose names I could never remember.'

Flower and David were to become part of the new elite that was formed after India's independence. When the new government required that foreign companies should be jointly owned and managed, many well-placed Indians, including several Jews, stepped into coveted managerial and executive positions in foreign companies. Along with their newly acquired positions came all the associated colonial-style perks—homes, servants, club membership, and a higher social status. In this way more Indian men, including Jews, joined the ranks of the 'burra saabs' (big bosses) as heads and senior executives of large British firms. In proper colonial style their wives became 'burra mems' (wives of big bosses). Some large residences of departing Britishers were made available to those who could afford to purchase them. My parents and a few other affluent Jews capitalized on these opportunities. In 1955 they moved into a large, airy flat in Halwasiya Mansions on Moira Street, a desirable downtown location. The flat was an executive suite that belonged to the National and Grindlays Bank. The ten spacious flats in the building underwent a gradual change of residents as they became home to Hindu, Parsi, and Jewish families in the fifties. The foreign exchange business called for a great deal of entertaining. My parents entertained almost weekly and were out at parties most nights of the week. Their Moira Street flat was very spacious and they had the necessary domestic help to accommodate this lifestyle. It is here, on Moira Street, that the story of my life begins.

Notes

Flyleaf: Flower in 1945, outside her home in Tottee Lane.

1 Flower was the Anglicized version of her name and the one by which her parents called her. She was named after her grandmother Farha.

2 In the 1850s there were less than 500 Jews in Calcutta according to Musleah, *On the Banks of the Ganga*, p. 420. By the mid-twentieth century the accounts regarding the number of Jews in Calcutta fluctuate between Census reports that indicate that there were 2000 Jews, to other reports that there were 4000 Jews when the community was at its peak. In the early 1950s there were a number of Jewish refugees from Burma and other parts of the world who swelled the community temporarily. By the end of the twentieth century the numbers dwindled considerably leaving only a few hundred Jews in Calcutta at the turn of the century.

3 Sally Solomon's memoir, *Hooghly Tales*, is especially valuable for its depiction of the attitudes and emotions associated with everyday life in the community.

4 Solomon, in *Hooghly Tales*, comments on the relationship that Jews often had with their servants, acknowledging that 'good and trustworthy domestic staff played a large role in the running of [our] household [s].' In my discussion of the role of domestic workers in Jewish homes, I have drawn on Solomon's work as well as my own understanding of servant–employer relationships, familiar from my growing up in a household which depended on the work of several servants. Although my account is inevitably through an employer's eye, I strive to develop a critical analysis of this set of relationships.

5 Memmi, in *The Colonizer and the Colonized*, noted the typical colonizer's response to domestics: 'You can't count on them,' or 'they,' as a collective, 'are like this'. The use of the depersonalized plural further undermined the colonized and robbed the individual of his/her personhood.

6 In *Hooghly Tales*, Solomon records the nostalgia that the Jews felt towards their servants when they left India: 'Years could pass . . . yet time and time again, in colonial nostalgia, servants names invariably crop up. Remember Thomas? Kuppuswamy? Mary and Millie? Murumah . . . the list is endless, as are the anecdotes inseparable from each name; good or

bad, clever or cunning, servants made an indelible mark on our lives.'
Solomon then goes on to acknowledge the emotional dependence on servants. She quotes an older women who speaks of how lonely she is in
London: 'One could never be lonely in India. There were always the servants' (p. 21).

7 My mother helped find our ayah Pauline a job in London as an au pair.
She now lives in London with her daughter Elizabeth, who is a couple
of years younger than me, and has a professional job in London. Pauline
is still in touch with several Calcutta Jews who live there.

8 Patricia Hill Collins in *Black Feminist Thought: Knowledge, Consciousness and
the Politics of Empowerment* (New York/London: Routledge, 1990), quotes
Judith Rollins in her discussion of domestic work and its characteristics.
She argues that domestic work is more exploitative than other occupa-
tions. While Collins and Rollins are referring to the condition of Black
domestic workers in the United States, many of the characteristics of the
workplace and the nature of the relationship between employer and
domestic worker apply to domestic workers in general (pp. 55–8).

9 The Jewish Girls' School flourished, while the Talmud Torah did not
have as high an educational standard and reputation. Thus the boys from
many middle-class Jewish families, including Flower's brothers, attended
several of the Anglo-Indian schools in Calcutta such as Calcutta Boys'
School, La Martiniere, Saint Joseph's and St. Xavier's and a few even
went to boarding schools in the hills.

10 For example, during the Bengal Famine of 1943, the League made their
financial assistance available for the feeding of the destitute (Musleah, *On
the Banks of the Ganga*, p. 324). Destitute refugees from Europe throughout the thirties relied on assistance from the League.

11 Flower recalls having had to carbon copy each sheet of her examination five times to ensure that a copy of the paper would reach
Cambridge. Each set of papers was sent separately to avoid them being
lost. Story has it that at least three lots of papers never made it to
Cambridge and so the examination results were very delayed.

12 Solomon, *Hooghly Tales*, p. 121.

13 Appadurai, 'Here and Now' in *Modernity at Large*, p. 3.

14 Solomon, *Hooghly Tales*, p. 128.

15 Hannah Sen was the daughter of Abhijit Guha, a leading lawyer in nineteenth century Calcutta who married a Baghdadi Jewish woman. He con-

verted to Judaism and raised his two daughters, Hannah and Regina, as Jews. Both daughters led influential lives. Hannah did not marry a Jew as he had wished. She married Dr Arun Sen, a leading physician in Delhi, who was a Hindu. However, Hannah Sen was active in the Indian women's movement and in Jewish affairs.

16 Radha Kumar, *History of Doing* (London: Verso, 1993), p. 68. For a more detailed history of the Indian Women's Movement and the role of the AIWC see Jana Matson Everett, *Women and Social Change in India* (New Delhi: Heritage, 1979).

17 Prior to this period, in an attempt to embrace women from many different communities, AIWC's focus had been on broader women's issues. After considerable tension and debate within the organization, AIWC embraced the nationalist cause. This alienated those members who were not Congress supporters.

18 Kumar, *History of Doing*, p. 83.

19 For more on this topic see Mushirul Hasan (ed.), *India's Partition: Process, Strategy and Mobilization* (New Delhi: Oxford University Press, 1993).

20 Gandhi, who had great respect for all religions, declared 'I am a Hindu, a Muslim, a Christian, a Zoroastrian, a Jew.'

21 Faiz Ahmed Faiz in his poem 'Freedom's Dawn' speaks eloquently of the agony and uncertainty that many experienced as the country was sundered. Many in India felt a deep sense of loss.

> This leprous daybreak, dawn night's fangs have mangled—
> This is not that long-looked-for break of day.
> Not that clear dawn in quest of which those comrades
> Set out, believing that in heaven's wide void
> Somewhere must be the star's last halting place,
> Somewhere the verge of night's slow-washing tide,
> Somewhere an anchorage for the ship of heartache [. . .]
> But now, word goes, the birth of day from darkness
> Is finished, wandering feet stand at their goal;
> Our leaders' ways are altering, festive looks
> Are all the fashion, discontent reproved;—
> And yet this psychic still on unslaked eye

Or heart fevered by severance works no cure.

Where did that fine breeze, that the wayside lamp

Has not once felt, blow from——where has it fled?

Night's heaviness is unlessened still, the hour

Of mind and spirit ransom has not struck;

Let us go on, our goal is not reached yet.

The translation of this Urdu poem is taken from Sugato Bose and Ayesha Jalal, *Modern South Asia; History, Culture, Political Economy* (Delhi: Oxford University, 1999), p. 200.

22 The fate of Kashmir was determined after Partition and is still a source of tension between India and Pakistan. At independence, three-quarters of Kashmir's population was Muslim but its Maharaja, Hari Singh, was Dogra Hindu Rajput. The Dogra Rajput clan of Jammu ruled Kashmir with the assistance of Kashmiri brahman civil servants, the Pandits, whose most famous family was the Nehru-Kaul clan. When Britain was to transfer power Hari Singh was not able to accept accession to either India or Pakistan, and hoped Kashmir would be permitted to retain independence. As Muslim peasants in the southwest corner of the kingdom revolted against Dogra Rajput landowners and gained support from Pakistani Muslims, Hari Singh turned to Delhi for support. On 26 October Hari Singh acceded to India and requested support to defend Srinagar as tribal soldiers entered Kashmir. Mountbatten insisted, and Indian leaders agreed, that after the raiders had been driven out a plebiscite would be held—considering that the population was predominantly Muslim—regarding Kashmir's accession to India. Due to the Indian army intervention, tribal forces from Pakistan were repulsed. The fighting in Kashmir raged on until the state's de facto partition was effected. Azad Kashmir, a part of Kashmir, acceded to Pakistan. No plebiscite was ever held in Kashmir.

23 Stanley Wolpert, *A New History of India* (New York: Oxford University Press, 1993), p. 355.

24 Ibid.

25 Other Jewish women like Hannah Sen and her sister Regina were also active in Indian politics and became leaders. Their being Jewish was not a hindrance to their participation and attaining high office. Similarly, later General Jacob, also from the Baghdadi community, rose to be a General

in the Army and then to be Governor of Goa (1998) and his Jewishness was never an issue.

26 Musleah, *On the Banks of the Ganga,* p. 23.

27 Tharoor (ed.), *Naari,* p. 9.

28 Musleah, in *On the Banks of the Ganga* describes the entries in his diary. He notes the breadth of his interests and describes him as 'remarkably enlightened and cultured' (p. 24).

Jael:
Indian Portrait, Jewish Frame

$\mathscr{I}$ WAS BORN IN 1955, the third of Flower and David Silliman's five children, and I grew up as part of the Calcutta elite. Ever since I can remember, I considered myself Indian, as did my parents. Although they were proud of being Jewish, our home was not very Jewish. I would say we were outwardly Jewish rather than being really Jewish; by this I mean that our Jewishness was avowed rather than a lived experience. By the mid-1950s it had become difficult to carry out the basic rituals of Jewish life in Calcutta. For example, my parents could not find a mohel in Calcutta to perform the brit of their first child, Albert. A mohel had to be flown out from Bombay several days after Albert was born so that three brits could be performed on the same day (the rest of us children were girls so this particular problem did not resurface!).

My father proclaimed his Jewishness by closing his office on the Sabbath, and each Saturday he would don a hat for his wanderings around town. (The hats have become more flamboyant over the years: you could see him roaming around Calcutta on his Honda Cub motorbike sporting a sombrero, a Mughal-styled turban or a fez.) There is a mezuzah (blessing) on the front door of our apartment on Moira Street, and Friday night prayers and dinners were among the other public displays and pronouncements of Jewishness. Before we performed the prayers, my parents would explain the significance of the Sabbath to our guests and interpret the prayers. After kiddush and the breaking of the bread we all sat down to an elaborate, traditional Iraqi Jewish dinner.

Despite these outward markers of Jewishness, we did not follow the spirit or the letter of the law in our daily lives. I do remember my parents reminding us to say our *shema* before going to bed but I knew very little about the Jewish religion and practice. My grandmother Mary taught me how to read Hebrew, but I never understood the meaning of what I read, though I dutifully rattled off my *shema* each night and morning when I awoke. She also supervised Albert's preparation for his bar mitzvah, and made the Jewish festivals special for us with stories about the festival and treats and presents for the occasion. Once in a rare while she was successful in enticing us to attend a Saturday morning service in the Shaare Rason prayer hall she attended. I went a few times with Granny and got through what seemed to be interminably long services by counting the little printed flowers on the window curtains.

Granny would come at about four in the afternoon each Tuesday and sit primly in the verandah talking with Mummy and children—when we were around—as her crochet needles clicked rapidly. To me she seemed hopelessly old-fashioned in her calf-length, dowdy dresses and her quaint manner of speaking: '*Insh'Allah*, darling,' (which means 'God willing' in Arabic) or 'from your lips to God's ears,' as she would say when we shared our wishes with her. I never thought of Granny as anything else but Jewish: Jewishness just filled up her life and defined her. She would never eat anything in our non-kosher home and even sipped her own water from the flask she brought along with her on each visit. Even at that time the older Jewish people like Granny and her world seemed anachronistic. They seemed out of place to me in Calcutta—though they themselves felt perfectly at home.

By the 1960s there were only a handful of Jews left in Calcutta and the numbers dwindled with each passing year. My family was barely involved in whatever was left of Jewish community life. The few Jews we mixed with were like us—very assimilated Jews who lived on the periphery of the community. Several of my father's sisters had married Hindus and had further assimilated. We were close to two of my father's sisters and their families, Aunt Sybil and Aunt Esther, who had married a Bengali and a Sindhi respectively, and moved in social circles similar to ours. Their children, Shonanda, Sudeshna, Tina and Pia often celebrated Jewish festivals in our home. We had a set of more conservative Jewish cousins but we did not see them except at synagogue on the high holidays.

Though Jewishness was not part of my everyday life, it fixed my location in a very plural society. When people asked me what I was, I knew they were asking me to which community I belonged. I would be quick to respond: 'I am Jewish,' and they would know how to place me. Our Jewishness set us apart, made us different from others, and made us like the others around us. All my friends who were Indian like me, were also something else. They either identified themselves as Hindu, Muslim, Christian, Parsi or as Bengali, Punjabi or Marwari. All of us belonged to some community, even if only in name. We were all Indian, though the gods we followed, the festivals we celebrated, and the languages our ancestors spoke were distinct.

Our house on Moira Street had neither an Indian nor a Jewish flavour. We had few, if any, Indian artefacts—this was not yet the period of ethnic chic, which came into its own in the 1980s and 1990s when some upper-class Indians 'discovered' Indian artefacts. Rather, the decor was decidedly cosmopolitan and Western, and not that different from the homes of my affluent and Westernized Indian friends. They too had the same kind of Chesterfield sofas, English-style carpets, cutglass or crystal vases and dark wood dining room sets with matching sideboards. My parents and my siblings had some Jewish friends, but it so happened that there were no Jewish children my age among the few Jews in our circle. Mum and Dad had mostly Hindu, Parsi and a few Anglo-Indian friends. My father worked with several foreign bankers and entertained them regularly. I remember these parties in our home as rather posh affairs where my parents were keen to impress their guests. My mother made sure that the bearers' white uniforms were well-pressed, the silver polished, and the flowers arranged dramatically for maximum effect. My parents entertained or went about thrice a week to business parties, fancily dressed for the occasion. I recall admiring my mother's long evening dresses or the elegant silk saris she wore.

To my mother the relentless social life they led seemed like an 'endless round of cocktail parties', and she tired of it quickly. She wanted a profession, and my father encouraged her to work as a school teacher. This was considered a 'respectable' profession for a woman of means. After teaching home science and human biology in several schools in Calcutta, my mother decided she would go and live in London for a year to test the waters and see whether it would be a good idea for our family to emigrate to England. By this time several members of her family lived in London and the West still had an allure for her as a 'place of wide horizons'. To her the West represented:

Places where we could go beyond the little Jewish world of Calcutta, where we could be part of a larger English-speaking world, where there were many more Jews of different cultures, and where we could be part of those larger communities. The West was the world we had seen in the movies, in the books we read, and it looked attractive, inviting, and extremely comfortable. It seemed so modern with machines, and fast-moving inter-city trains, while we lived in an old-fashioned world of rickshaws, trams, and crowded buses. The West seemed like a place where we could get good jobs, where our language and education would work to our advantage. The sights and places, the shops that were in our imagination, would become real.

My mother, Granny, and us children (there were four of us now) lived in Golders Green, London, from 1960-61. Mum taught at a school in Edgeware. After experiencing the West as a working woman and mother, however, she came to appreciate her life in Calcutta. She speaks candidly of her privileged lifestyle and her reluctance to give it up: 'Living in London posed a great challenge. I was suddenly a working woman, teaching at school, taking the subway, looking after kids, cooking, shopping, and running a household minus all the Indian servants I was used to having. Did I really want to relinquish the position of 'burra memsaab' in Calcutta to settle in London?' She decided it would not be a good idea for the family to emigrate, so we returned to Calcutta. Granny decided to stay on in London.

On returning from London my mother found a job as a teacher at Loreto House. Formerly, it had been a school for upper-class British and Anglo-Indian children, with a handful of elite Armenians, Jews, and Indians. After independence Loreto House catered to upper-class Indian students and some Anglo-Indian and Indian Catholics. By the 1960s Loreto House had mostly Indian teachers, but there were some Anglo-Indian, British, and Armenian teachers left. A few Irish nuns headed the school's administration, but the majority of the nuns were Indian. Right through the 1960s and 1970s the Loreto nuns wore the Western long white habit, black veil, and white wimple. (Today, when I go back to visit, I find it odd to see the nuns dressed in their shorter habits or in saris.)

The missionary schools had clear instructions from the government that they were not to proselytize, and they had to follow an Indian curriculum.

Thus, though the language of instruction at Loreto House was English, Hindi and Bengali were compulsory second languages. Many of the Indian students came from Anglicized families and spoke English at home. Flower taught home science and health science and was known for her quick wit and firm discipline. She was active in all the school's extra-curricular activities, including taking her class regularly to volunteer at Mother Teresa's newly opened orphanage Shishu Bhavan. At Loreto, Flower often thwarted the rules. To the chagrin of the nuns she was the first teacher to wear pants to school and others cautiously followed suit. She was not flustered or embarrassed as she explained the details of human anatomy and the human reproductive process to her wide-eyed students. She openly smoked cigarettes during the break in her home science room. Flower felt very much in command at Loreto House.

Mum spent her days in school and in the late afternoons she saw to the running of our home. In the evenings she was busy getting dressed and ready for business entertaining. When she attended Indian functions, she often wore Western formal clothes and when she went to European functions she usually wore a sari. She explains why:

> At predominantly Indian functions I felt the saris and jewellery I wore were no match for the expensive traditional saris that many women of this class had inherited along with their exquisite jewellery. However, in Western clothes I would not compare unfavourably with them. At predominantly European functions I enjoyed wearing saris, which were much appreciated and admired. Similarly, at the parties I threw I would have the cook prepare Iraqi and Western food for my Indian and European colleagues, which was a unique combination.

Mum often taught Indian bankers' wives how to entertain Western style, cook Western foóds, or decorate their homes in more 'modern' ways. She shared Indian culture, recipes, social etiquette and general know-how about the city with the wives of foreign bankers who were interested in getting to know India. She was very comfortable in the role of go-between. She kept in close touch with many of her Indian, Parsi, and Anglo-Indian friends from her school and college years. At Loreto she was friendly with many of the teachers who came from the Hindu, Muslim, Parsi, and the Anglo-Indian communities.

We children attended Loreto House and La Martiniere Boys' school.

By this time the Jewish Girls' School had lost its high standard. Since there were very few Jews left in Calcutta, we mixed mostly with Indian children in school and at home. We had a handful of Jewish friends who were in school with us or were neighbours or relatives. We enjoyed all the amenities of upper-class life in Calcutta. I would walk to the Calcutta Club of which my father is a member, and spend hours swimming, playing tennis, and generally hanging around there. The colonnaded mansion, with deep marble verandahs, is set in the heart of Calcutta amidst green lawns, and grass courts for tennis. The 'bearers' (or waiters) had brass numbers pinned onto their white starched uniforms so you could call out to them without having to know their names. My father is among the few members to address them by name as they take down his order. After a swim, I took it for granted that the club ayahs would help me brush and dry my hair and generally pick up after me. I would order and sign, using my father's club membership number, for *pakoras*, ice-creams and cold drinks which the bearers would serve me and my friends on the verandah of the swimming pool or on the lawn. My father would pay the quite steep club bills at the end of the month and rarely question us about the items we generously signed for in his name.

We travelled for holidays mostly to Gopalpur, a seaside resort in Orissa, and to other parts of India. We went abroad to England a couple of times by cargo ship. My father had arranged foreign exchange for the purchase of ships by the India Steamship Company. Thereafter the owner offered him the owner's suite on board their ships should he or his family wish to travel. My mother and grandmother and we children made two such trips to Europe that took several months to complete. On one voyage, when I was five years old, the ship was carrying a rickshaw, a load of birds and thirteen baby elephants to the Bertram Mills Circus in England! I remember bathing and walking the elephants around the deck between the holds and helping the crew out with the chores. We fed the elephants sugarcane and bananas. I have a fleeting memory of elephants trumpeting with their limbs wide apart as they were hoisted by crane on to the ship.

In many ways, my world was very small. I took my privilege for granted, was blissfully unaware of politics, and uncritical of the classism and sexism that infused my social world. I grew up in the 1960s and 1970s in an in-between space—not traditionally Indian, but not truly Western either. The West was not part of my imagination, in part because India's blend of Gandhian and Socialist policies kept Western products and companies out of India from 1947 till the late eighties, when liberalism gained a foothold. Although I lived in London for a year when I was five, I only remember it from the photographs and the old home movies. I was about fourteen when we went to England again to visit my brother and sister who were at school in Wales. On that trip I remember the novelty of buying a few things and bringing them back, but the West was not a cultural reference point as it had been for my Mum's generation. I wore Western clothes that the durzees made, and I bought ready-made kurtas. At fifteen and six- teen I remember wearing a *lungi* (a type of sarong) that was very fashion- able at the time, teamed with a kurta. We took our fashion cues from what other Westernized Indians were wearing.

During the time I was growing up, only a few English and Hollywood movies came to Calcutta theatres. While Bollywood (Bombay-made Hindi) films were popular, my friends and I had little interest in them, though I do remember seeing three or four big hit films and knew some film songs. From the age of about ten to thirteen, I saw Western films in the home of Bill Lichtman, whom we all called Uncle Bill. Uncle Bill was an American-Jewish burra saab of a shipping company who lived in Calcutta for many years. He loved children and opened his large garden home to children and teenagers every Sunday evening. About a hundred of us would arrive at around six in the evening to feast on sandwiches, cakes, and sodas that were laid out for us. After this high tea we would seat ourselves on the carpet and sofas in his large hall to see cartoons and a movie on a screen. I remember seeing cowboy movies but we also saw classics like *Sabrina* and *Seven Brides for Seven Brothers*. After the movie we lined up and Uncle Bill doled out two silver-paper wrapped chocolates to each of us before we went home. Looking back, I find it curious that I knew so lit- tle about Uncle Bill. I looked forward to going there to see friends and enjoy the movies and just thought of him as a kindly old man who loved children.

My gregarious father would often bring people home to visit. As a child I never knew who would be turning up for dinner or how long they would stay. One day my father would be deeply engrossed in conversation with a Catholic, Armenian, or Protestant priest, the next he would be extending hospitality to a hippie he had just met in the New Market at Nahoum's shop and whom he brought home for a meal or to stay with us for a while.[1] In the 1960s my parents listed our name and address in the tourist office as a place where Jews visiting Calcutta could come for a

Sabbath meal. This added to the already heavy traffic in and out of the house. Dad entertained the foreign visitors and took them around town because he was bent on shattering stereotypes about Calcutta. Many of these transient visitors, Jews and non-Jews alike, stayed with us for a few days or weeks at a time. Some would be so comfortable that they would stay a few months. Danny, an Israeli visitor, stayed with us a whole year. My parents thought it would be a good way for us to learn some spoken Hebrew, but instead we taught Danny how to speak English. He never became proficient at reading or writing, though at the end of his stay he announced, with Israeli chutzpah, that he was going to teach English in Japan.

Harold, a Jew from New York, who claimed to be the first Buddhist Jew, is among the more memorable visitors to our home. Harold used our house as a base for his various visits to Buddhist holy places. After one such pilgrimage he returned with his long frizzy hair infested with lice. I remember Mummy—first politely and persuasively, and then sternly—telling him that he needed to disinfect himself. Waving him in the direction of the bathroom, she handed him a bar of carbolic soap and a bottle of blue ointment, and insisted he proceed with the treatment right away. Harold hesitated. He wanted to know the fate of the creatures exposed to such a regimen. To our amazement, the otherwise pacific Buddhist Jew declared firmly that he would not kill a living being. By this time Mummy was totally exasperated and told Harold, in no uncertain terms, that if he did not agree to her terms he and his lice would have to find another place to live. So Harold's visit ended abruptly and unceremoniously. Mum and I still laugh as we recall this incident.

A truly motley bunch passed through our home—Mum always declared that each was a *namuna* (one of a kind). For the most part I enjoyed meeting these characters, but I was too busy with my own life to pay them much attention. To me all these folks seemed foreign and different from us—people who were passing through but not a part of my life. They were much older than me, so I found even less in common with them. I did enjoy listening to their stories and their perceptions of life in Calcutta, but never found a place for them in my world, which was filled with my own friends and school activities.

Our lifestyle, with the constant flow of guests in and out of the house, depended on servants—a full-time ayah, a cook, a boy and a part-time sweeper—who made it possible for our busy household to cater to every-one's demands. My parents could go out and entertain regularly because the servants looked after us children, kept the home running, and cooked meals for the family and guests. There was a strict hierarchy among the servants who worked in our home about what chores each one would and would not do. I remember, for instance, when the sweeper was not there, we would have to make arrangements for another sweeper in the building to wash and polish the floor. It was considered beneath the dignity of the other servants to take on this task. It was only by the mid to late 1970s, when it was becoming harder to get reliable household help, that one ser-vant would be hired to help with multiple tasks, though a part-time sweep-er was still necessary. Though my parents did remind us to be considerate of the servants, and did provide them with days off from work, their lives were structured around us, our whims, our moods and our desires. After playing or a late night party, we went to bed leaving the house in a mess, knowing full well that when we awoke it would be neat. The ayah sleep-ing on a mat on our bedroom floor was expected to ignore the noise we made. There was no space where she could be alone or away from the constant bustle in the house. I feel ashamed that I never thought of this incessant entertaining at their expense, or their complete lack of space, as an injustice.

During my last two school years (1969-71) the Jesuit priests and nuns who were committed to reducing poverty awakened my interest in social justice issues. I participated in many social service projects and took it upon myself to teach some of the servants' children how to read English. I remember the stern reprimands of Kanchi, my ayah at that time, and the cook, Chand Muhammad (by this time Karmalli had retired), who thought it improper for me to teach the liftman's son, who was a few years older than me. Furthermore, they said, by coming up to the apartment and sit-ting with me, he might get uppity ideas. I defiantly replied that my par-ents did not object to my teaching him and they need not worry about my reputation. What I did not realize was that our behaviour tarnished the ser-vant's reputation among the other servants in the building. The liftman's son, as well as the other servants' children, continued to come up to the house to study. I would sit on the bed and they would squat on the floor at my feet. I sometimes sat down on the floor with them but it never crossed my mind to go down to the servants' quarters to teach them.

I have never been inside the quarters, though I often looked down at them through my bedroom window—a two-storeyed concrete structure with a line of small rooms on each floor opening onto a narrow verandah. Each room in the quarter belonged to a particular flat, housing a servant and his family. The ten families all shared a common toilet. I casually watched the children play in the back compound, saw the men sit out, smoking and chatting at the end of the day while their wives took care of the children, cooked meals, swept, and fetched water. I did not question the fact that their lives and mine would rarely intersect—we lived different lives in different worlds, even though we shared a common compound.

Not only was I detached from the lives of those people who worked for us, I was also mostly unaware of the Naxalite Movement in Calcutta and the surrounding districts, which was at its peak in the late 1960s and the 1970s. Calcutta was a stronghold of the Communist Party of India Marxist (CPI-M), and the Naxalites, who adopted a more Maoist line, broke from the party to form the CPI Marxist-Leninist (CPI-ML). The Naxalites, who were committed to armed agrarian revolution, built a base in the countryside. During 1970–71 there was a great deal of Naxal activity in Calcutta. The Government, through the Central Reserve Police, local police and the army mounted a systematic campaign of arrest, torture and shooting in Calcutta and its immediate vicinities. While I knew of Naxalites and I had heard of a few people in our social circles whose sons or brothers were involved in Naxal activities, I knew nothing about the political philosophy that guided this movement. I do not recall our ever discussing the Naxalites in school, either in our lessons or in conversation. Although the movement was all around us it was not part of our world. While the priests and nuns acquainted us with the injustices of poverty, they did not address the political processes that produce poverty, nor the political philosophies that challenge it.

The Anglicized and more privileged parts of the city where I lived, went to school and played, was a world apart from these political events. We heard about what was happening through *The Statesman* (an English-language newspaper) and from the hartals (strikes), bandhs (shut-downs), and gheraos (workers' barricades) that peaked in the late 1960s and early 1970s and became daily occurrences. Sometimes these troubles, that for the most part were kept at bay, spilled over into our worlds. A father of a very close friend of mine, and the secretary of an elite club, was killed in one such random act of 'terrorism' against the rich. The parents of my friends and my father's colleagues complained about the 'terrorists' (which is how they described Naxalites), discussed the labour troubles, and bemoaned the flight of industry from the city. Most people we knew were Congress supporters and had no sympathy for nor interest in radical politics. Reflecting my class background, subliminally, I had very centrist politics, if they could be called politics at all.

I did not get caught up in the revolutionary political currents that engulfed a large part of Calcutta. I was more aware of the civil war across the border, which had become somewhat of a family matter. In my last year of school, 1971, the Indian army, with my paternal grand-uncle General J. F. R. Jacob as its chief strategist, 'liberated' Bangladesh.[2] My carefree childhood was most heavily clouded by the tensions between my parents. I tried to shut their increasingly troubled marriage out of my life as much as possible. Though frequently embarrassed about their fighting, especially when they fought in front of my friends, and disturbed by the shouting and threats that they hurled at each other, I went on with my life. I was out of the house a lot, and when I was there I always had friends over who knew what was going on at home. My mother offers a brief account of the deterioration of her marriage:

> David and I grew apart in the second decade of our marriage. We had very different tastes and lifestyles that were exacerbated over time. Both of us were strong personalities and found it difficult to adapt to each other's values and tastes. David was also a heavy drinker, liked big crowds and parties and constant entertainment. This life of constant partying and drinking did not appeal to me. The marriage continued in name because we had five children and he would not let me leave with them. Therefore we lived very separate lives, which was a source of great pain to me. We did, however, keep up social appearances of being together. This was the done thing in our circle.

My parents did agree that their children should go abroad to study after finishing school in Calcutta. Although the exorbitant expenses of a foreign education, and foreign exchange restrictions, made it an uphill task for my father to provide this opportunity for all five of us while still maintaining the high standard of living at home, our parents felt that studying at a university abroad would give us better educational and career opportunities. They also hoped that living abroad would provide us with more possibilities to meet and marry Jews. Thus, after completing high school in

India, Esther and Albert, my elder sister and brother, went to Wales in the late 1960s for their A levels (advanced levels in the English school system). They then applied for and received scholarships to colleges in the United States. In the early 1970s I followed them to Britain after graduating from high school, and my younger sister, Michal, went to study in Israel. Lahava, the youngest, went to boarding school in Darjeeling for her last few years of high school. And so the family began to scatter.

Once the children had left home, my mother and father saw little reason to stay together and decided to get a divorce. In the past the contentious issue of custody over the children had always remained unresolved. It was not possible to get a legal Jewish divorce in Calcutta at that time, and so my mother decided to seek one in Israel, where she chose to stay rather than return to Calcutta. She explains her decision:

> I felt I wanted to make a new life in Israel now that I had got my freedom from David. Israel was a much more liberal environment than India for a divorced woman. In Calcutta it would have been difficult to live independently, as we moved in the same social circles. Two of my children were in Israel and I hoped that the younger ones would soon follow and I could be close to them.

Furthermore, as a divorced woman in India, Flower was not entitled to much financial maintenance from David, and it would have been hard for her to live on the small wages from her job at Loreto. While Loreto was an elite school, and the teachers, all women, had social status, they earned very little. This was typical of school teachers' wage structures at the time. Teachers like my mother, from upper-class families, rationalized it by saying 'they did not need the money'. Few women from such families worked, so teaching in school for many was a form of 'noblesse oblige'. She was confident that she would be able to support herself in another country, though she knew it would be hard at first. At the age of forty-eight, with a small settlement from David, Flower moved to Jerusalem.

Although Esther and Albert had already paved the way for me, my parents had made it clear that I would be sent abroad only if I performed reasonably well in my school-leaving exams. Much to our combined amazement, I did well and was sent abroad for my A levels. I looked forward to the new experience of studying and living abroad for a while, though my closest friends went on to study at colleges in India. It seemed like an adventure—my turn to see and experience the world. And so I left home in 1972, to stay in London for the summer before starting school in fall.

Even before leaving Calcutta I had to grapple for the first time with issues of race. My elder sister, Esther, is a lot darker than me and has straight black hair. I was disturbed to hear of her pain and humiliation at the racial slurs hurled at her by classmates in her boarding school in Wales. I had heard enough about racism in England to know that I did not want to go there, and we found out that I could do my A levels in Northern Ireland. The nuns in Calcutta assured my parents that despite the Irish 'troubles', Loreto College, Coleraine, was a safe place to send me.

I met racism as soon as I stepped off the plane in London, when an officious English woman rudely told all Indian passport holders to form a separate line and pushed and herded us to one side. I was raging, as I had never been treated in this manner before. When she approached me, about to shove me as she did the others, in a snooty but steady voice I told her to keep her hands off me. I let her know that I could follow instructions without being pushed around. For a moment she was startled, but my intervention had the desired effect—she almost politely asked me to stand aside. Ever since that moment I have made it a point to confront people on their racist behaviour.

I spent two years (1972-74) in Loreto College, Coleraine. I was extremely different from the other students. Since there were only about five foreign students at the school, we were considered 'exotic' and I did not experience any blatant racism. I was not aware enough to pick up on the more subtle and unintentional forms of racism towards me. These two years were socially, culturally, and politically bleak. I was starved for India. I constantly felt I had to explain who I was, and I developed a strong Irish lilt just to be understood. I missed my friends back in India and longed to be with people who were familiar. I dreamt of eating Indian food and going back home for a visit, but due to foreign exchange restrictions I could not return to India till four years after I first left home at sixteen.

A scholarship to the United States marked another very important moment in my life. Coming to the Boston area from my convent school experiences in Calcutta and Coleraine gave me an incredible sense of liberation and freedom. Just as my mother entered a new world when she left her Jewish environment in Calcutta and went to college in Delhi, I felt that being in Boston for college opened up the space for me to make choices for myself about who I was and what I wanted to be. My elder sister, Esther, had been very involved in Hillel and Jewish student activities on and off campus at Wellesley College, and went on to study at the Hebrew University of Jerusalem. My brother Albert was in his last year at Brandeis University, a predominantly Jewish school, and tellingly wrote in his yearbook: 'In India I was a Jew among Indians, at Brandeis I am an Indian among Jews.' His comment underlines how identity, which is relative and structured around difference, is often constructed by others as well as by oneself. Albert's succinct remark also underlines that identity cannot be merely an outcome of a process of selection but has to be constantly negotiated. When we came to the United States, each of us had to figure out who we were and what we wanted to be. It is interesting that we each negotiated very different primary identities for ourselves.

On arriving in the Boston area I instinctively identified with the South Asian diaspora that was only beginning to have a tentative foothold in the United States. I immediately sought out Indian students and in a matter of weeks made a circle of friends from the subcontinent, most of whom came from Westernized backgrounds similar to mine. For the most part they, too, had been educated in English-medium and elite schools. We hung around, as people from the subcontinent do, in groups (I was much more comfortable with this than dating and meeting people in parties and mixers), we visited each other, we cooked Indian food, went to the movies and socialized together. I felt at home with them. I also had other foreign student friends and a few White American friends. I did not try to fit into life in the United States because I believed I was just here to study and would go back to India when I got my degree.

In the United States I found myself inserted into a different world than I had experienced in Ireland. While both were predominantly White worlds, here I could choose to identify with non-Whites. I expanded my circle of friends beyond the South Asian community to include several African-American students. I learned directly and indirectly about racism and White privilege. While I was very familiar with class privilege in Calcutta, racism and its working in the United States was new to me. I took my first political science course with Manfred Maxneef, a charismatic dissident from Chile who supported Allende and opposed the Pinochet regime.[3] I enrolled in a class with Noam Chomsky and became interested in leftist politics. I was active in many South Asian student organizations where we read Marx in study groups and ran endless debates regarding whether India was a feudal, capitalist, or semi-capitalist society. We studied the development of political movements in India and critiqued the various party lines. The political analysis and grounding that I developed gave me the intellectual tools to understand contemporary political developments and deepened my understanding of the many ways in which social change can be realized. It laid a firm foundation for my intellectual development and focused my attention on the dynamics of movement building, which is a lasting interest.

It was also during my college years that I was introduced to feminism. This has remained an abiding and formative influence on my life. The first United Nations Conference on Women took place at Mexico City in 1975. My teacher, Carolyn Elliott, brought back the papers from the conference for us to review and discuss. I was from the outset impassioned by Third World women's movements and politics, took a keen interest in United States feminist politics, and participated in feminist activities on campus. I read and discussed new feminist books as they were published and was part of many feminist consciousness-raising groups.

As a result of my political awakening I returned to Calcutta in my junior year with very new views. I shared my socialist and feminist dreams and aspirations with my friends and was determined to work for social and gender justice in India. I became keenly conscious that the Calcutta I had known is one that only the privileged experience. This privilege, which I had taken for granted, became disconcerting. I was self-conscious and uneasy when I went with friends and my dad to the Calcutta Club. I saw it for what it was—one of the last bastions of colonialism. Ever since that time I have been painfully aware that my nostalgia about Calcutta is reactionary, my carefree, comfortable life there a function of my upper-class status. I have come to appreciate bell hooks's distinction between the 'useless act' of 'longing for something to be as once it was' and 'remembering that serves to illuminate the present'.[4] I hope this insight informs and tempers my nostalgia towards Calcutta.

On completing my degree in 1977, I returned to India to work at Seva Mandir, a non-governmental organization in Rajasthan. Seva Mandir was concerned with literacy and rural development and worked among tribal people in the district. Friends of mine introduced me to Dr Mohan Sinha Mehta, the founder of Seva Mandir, and he was happy to have me volunteer there. In the spirit of Gandhian voluntarism and service, but with leftist and feminist politics, I worked at Seva Mandir for a little over a year. Living in Udaipur was a completely new experience for me and brought me directly in touch with a very feudal rural India. The staff at Seva Mandir included Gandhians, socialists, leftists, feminists, and some who saw their work as nothing more than a secure job. I was assigned to work with Harijan (untouchable) children in a Harijan colony near the Lake Palace Hotel, as well as to work in a women's employment project in the city. At Seva Mandir I witnessed Gandhians trying to work with leftists and feminists, and the tensions and compromises of political accommodation. I admired many of the people working on social justice issues in the area and in India, and familiarized myself with their work. I was particularly interested in the work of the growing women's movement in India and the grassroots mobilization with which they were engaged. I remember inviting the labour organizer Ela Bhatt, who had recently formed the Self Employed Women's Association (SEWA), to speak to the women we were training in small-scale production activities. We were all mesmerized by her rousing speech about the need to unionize, and listened intently as she described her attempts to unionize workers in the non-formal sector. I also participated in several of the early meetings in Delhi where women organizers across India gathered to draft the Indian Report on the Status of Women for the United Nations Decade for Women (1975–85). In 1978 there was very little, by way of information and statistics, on women in India, but this United Nations call for women's involvement in development plans galvanized women's development projects and women's studies in India.

In Udaipur I dressed only in saris or in khadi (homespun) kurta and pajamas, and tried hard to improve my spoken and written Hindi. I worked amidst poor people and came to know and work alongside a lot of middle to lower middle-class people at Seva Mandir. This year in Udaipur was transformative because it was the first time I did not rely on my class privilege in India. While I had always known and seen poor people, I had never tried to empathize with them before. I witnessed hunger and poverty, as well as the petty jealousies, hypocrisies, and ego battles of people supposedly committed to serving the poor. I spent several months living with Ratna, a staff member of Seva Mandir, in her rundown family haveli (mansion) in the inner city of Udaipur. I paid her a small amount for room and board and shared her tiny room on the second floor of the dilapidated family house. Each unit of the extended family lived in one or two small rooms that overlooked the common courtyard. Ratna's old, widowed mother would cook for us each evening. At the end of our workday we would change and then go down to her room to eat. We would squat on the floor as she placed our thalis before us. She sat down beside us, serving and watching us eat. Though she would always offer us more food, I knew there was barely enough to go around, so I became used to staying hungry. There was no privacy in our lives—the only place in the house where people would not be disturbed was in the dark, smelly latrine shared by the entire family, that lay at the far corner of the courtyard. It had a pit and no running water or flush. I finally got accustomed to squatting there, and only after living there for a few months did I appreciate why people sat inside for what seemed to be long intervals—it was the only place where they could have privacy.

These quarters were not that different from those of the domestic workers in my Calcutta home. For this brief time I bridged the social and material gulf that separated me from the majority. I could only do this far away from my home in Calcutta, in a place where nobody knew me or where I came from. People knew that I was privileged and different from them—someone passing through. I could live like this because it was my choice to have this experience. So, for a year I fleetingly glimpsed poverty and discrimination from that insider/outsider position where I often find myself. I did not, however, experience a poor person's crushing realization of the near impossibility of escaping from poverty. That year in Rajasthan made me understand at a very gut level the processes that produce and sustain poverty and injustice—it was another understanding that has stayed with me. I believe that year in Rajasthan was the furthest I have travelled in coming to know and experience closely the lives of people so different from me, across class lines. In a sense, it was much like my mother's trip to Delhi, where she immersed herself in the lives of her fellow Indian students. This travel experience—which could be described as vertical—has had the most profound, lasting impact. It dwarfs my travel experiences across countries and continents.

During this time in my life when I was self-consciously adopting a political Indian identity, several members of my family were leaving India. My mother had just left India in 1978 and was trying to find her place in Israel. She enrolled in an ulpan (a full-time Hebrew school where one learns through immersion in the language) for six months in Jerusalem and acquainted herself with life in Israel. She chose Jerusalem because there were many English-speaking immigrants (Anglo-Saxons) living there. Flower was not used to and was unwilling to accept a working-class lifestyle and found it very hard to adjust to a much lower financial status. She took a few years to establish a set of friends whom she considered her social equals. After a few years she capitalized on both her Indian identity and her culinary skills to start the Maharaja restaurant.

The Maharaja, in downtown Jerusalem, was the first kosher non-vegetarian Indian restaurant in the world and this unique feature made for a lot of publicity. The restaurant was reviewed favourably in many papers internationally and even got a small write up in the *New York Times*. Tourists—especially those who were kosher and liked Indian food but could only eat in vegetarian Indian restaurants—along with some regular customers from Jerusalem, were her primary clientele. Cochini and Bene Israeli Jews from Tel Aviv and Ramleh often hired the restaurant for bar mitzvahs. Their guests gathered for an Indian lunch at the Maharaja after they concluded the prayers at the Wailing Wall, which was not far away. Mum welcomed them, as they conducted the celebrations drawing on both traditionally Indian and Israeli customs. Many celebrities came to the restaurant, including Zubin Mehta, the celebrated conductor of the Israeli Philharmonic Orchestra, a Parsi, who, mum says 'brought the Maharaja prestige by his patronage'.

As my family was relocating, I thought I should spend a few years in Israel. I helped my mother out in the restaurant while I joined an ulpan and familiarized myself with Arab-Israeli politics and the organizing traditions of the Israeli Left. I became very close friends with Najib, a Palestinian student from the United States, who was studying in Israel. Through him I understood the daily difficulties of living as a Palestininian in a Jewish state and the tensions and fears in both communities regarding those who 'cross the line'. I joined the political science department at the Hebrew University but found it too much of an uphill struggle to study in Hebrew. While I waited several months for my student visa to return to graduate school in the United States, I worked as a maid cleaning rooms in a hotel in Eilat, where the foreign guests assumed I was an Arab worker. One guest asked me which Arab village I came from, and a few were blatantly racist. Sometimes they spoke in English about me in my presence, assuming I could not understand what they were saying. Though I was very aware of the discrimination against Arab workers in Israeli society, I had little interest in countering racist and classist attitudes. I think this was because I was to leave Israel shortly.

Back in the United States for graduate school, I focused on issues of gender and economic development. I met Amitava, an Indian student from a traditional, lower middle-class Bengali brahman family that had become middle-class over the years. Simply put, we would have never met each other in Calcutta, as we come from different worlds. When I talked about Calcutta, he would listen to my stories with amazement because they did not seem to be about a Calcutta he knew. I was equally intrigued to hear about his strict and very traditional upbringing. Ever since he left Calcutta for college in Kharagpur, Amitava was eager to encounter and learn about new intellectual and cultural traditions. We married in 1981, when I still hoped to return to India. He agreed to return with me if he found a professionally fulfilling position.

At this stage in my life I knew and cared little about United States politics, as I felt I was just passing through—I definitely still considered myself a foreign student. In fact, during the first two years of our marriage my head was filled with the desire to return to India permanently, and I made plans and arrangements towards that goal after Amitava had completed his two-year post-doctoral appointment. Though there was not a large Indian community at that time, we made several Indian friends and spent time with them when we were not working and studying. We especially enjoyed the Indian friends who were politically committed like us, and discussed Indian politics at length. We returned to India for a year and our daughter Shikha was born in Bombay (now Mumbai) during our last few months in India. My mother came from Israel for her birth and my in-laws did all the appropriate pujas for her. We also performed a Jewish naming ceremony. In 1984, when Shikha was barely three months old, we returned to the United States, not knowing what the future held in store for us. Amitava threw himself into his work but I was rudderless—I had organized my life and studies to work in India. I now had to make a life for myself in the States, but I was not emotionally ready to let go of India completely. However, having made the commitment to live in the United States I found political communities with which to engage and so began to find my place and voice.

Feminism had been important to me since my years as a college student but I had identified primarily with third world women's movements and struggles for social change. I was familiar with feminist political

Above The next generation: *(left)* Maya in traditional classical Indian bharat natyam dance costume and *(right)* Shikha in Indian dress, with her mother. *Below* Jael and Flower at a rally.

activism in India but had not sought out a location for myself in United States feminist circles. In the United States I came to identify as a 'woman of colour' and a Third World feminist. By this I mean I am committed to the materialist feminist philosophy that refuses to disengage the economic and social rights of women from the individual and bodily rights of women. As a Third World feminist I am committed to an anti-racist and anti-colonial perspective. I am active in transnational feminist as well as United States feminist organizing. I engage actively and participate with women's movements within and outside the United States and seek to highlight the voices of Third World women wherever they are located. In my lasting relationships with other feminists we together strive to reshape the world and make our voices heard. At a personal level feminist knowledge, perspectives and experiences give me the courage and confidence to question the status quo and to 'talk back'.[5]

I came to know United States politics and organizing traditions firsthand through my first job, which was as a programme officer in the Noyes Foundation, a progressive foundation in New York, committed to issues of the environment and population. When I joined the Foundation in the mid-eighties there was a great deal of organizing among people of colour in both the reproductive rights and the environmental movement, to expand these more mainstream agendas. I was very sympathetic to the critiques being launched by people of colour and learned about these issues through activists in the field, through site visits, grant-making and attending key conferences on these issues. Together with my colleagues at the Foundation I worked to introduce these perspectives in our grant making, and the Foundation became a leader on issues of environmental justice, the concerns of women of colour and reproductive rights.

In addition to participating in United States feminist and racial justice efforts, I learned more about feminist and environmental advocacy in Latin America through the Foundation's engagement there. Several trips to Latin America broadened my political understanding of this region of the world. I also reached out to participate in transnational feminist efforts to advance women's health and rights. Based in New York and working for a pro-active foundation I was ideally located to play an active role in the series of influential United Nations conferences (1990–95) that brought women's voices to bear on issues of population, human rights, and the environment. I was particularly active in the feminist organizing around the Rio Conference on Environment and Development, the Cairo Conference on

Population and Development and the Women's Conference in Beijing. During this period my network in transnational feminist movements broadened considerably.

At the Noyes Foundation, in addition to learning about these issues, expanding my political understanding of movements in the United States, and broadening my political networks, I gained very practical experience about how social change is fostered and forged in the States. I identified with the organizing efforts of women of colour and supported their efforts for social change. I became more knowledgeable and committed to issues of environmental justice and learned more about Native American sovereignty struggles. An entirely new world of activism opened up to me in this politically and intellectually exciting phase in my life. The issues that I worked on continue to shape my academic work and I have a strong commitment to bridging activism and scholarship.

Though I organize and identify as an immigrant and as a woman of colour, I am always conscious of the privileges I have by virtue of my upper-class background, my education, and my professional status. While I am a woman of colour and immigrant in the United States, I am aware that I do not share many of the experiences of oppression and prejudice that too many such women must confront and battle with on a daily basis. Whereas I organize as an Asian American and a Woman of Color in the racially and ethnically based politics of the United States, these are strategic and political identities. They do not capture the essence of who I am. The terms Asian American and Woman of Color only have valence and meaning within the United States and even there, these identities are of limited use; I do not share a common heritage or understanding with the experiences of a Lao immigrant, who, like me, is an Asian American. Nor do I identify with the experiences of an African American or Latina who, like me, is a 'woman of colour'. We have forged these political alliances because of our 'shared visions of a better society for all of us'.[6] We are allies who understand that by coming together we will learn from each other's differences, and that it is the only way we will be counted and heard in a dominant White society that still lumps us, all non-Whites, together. While organizing as a woman of colour is strategically important, being a woman of colour is not a primary identity for me. Being an Indian and a feminist define me more completely.

Though I have found a political home in the States, the pull of India remains strong. I am an active member of the South Asia Studies Program and write and teach about women's movements in India. I identify with the South Asian diaspora and identify with progressive movements in this rapidly expanding community. Amitava and I visit India regularly with the children. Our two daughters, Shikha and Maya (who was born in New Jersey in 1990) look forward to these trips. When they were young they celebrated Indian festivals and clapped along with my mother-in-law as she did her daily puja rituals, which Maya likened to playing dolls with her thakuma (Bengali for paternal grandmother). The children have experienced middle-class life in a Bengali family from staying with Amitava's parents. They have also spent time in my father's house and with my more elite, Anglicized friends and their children. They seem comfortable in both these very different Indian worlds and very at home in Iowa City.

I continue to learn about the United States through my appointment in Women's Studies at the University of Iowa, and I am involved in progressive feminist movement activities and organizations. In my classes I learn firsthand from my predominantly White American students about the challenges of growing up female. They share parts of their life with me in journals, discussion groups and meetings in my office. Immersed in work and family, with a greater understanding of politics, I have come to feel I am living in the United States. Still, when I visit Calcutta, my friends' children ask me about mainstream culture—the latest songs, fashions, and TV shows—and I never seem to know, since I do not watch television. I was really amused last visit when my friend's twelve-year-old son, not wanting to embarrass me, pulled me aside after the other children had left and asked: 'Jael Aunty, do you really live in America?' Despite his doubts, the United States is increasingly familiar and has become a second home. Amitava and I have just become United States citizens. We applied for citizenship after living in the United States for more than twenty years because we think we will be spending most of our lives here and want to be able to vote.

Just as my own life has been intertwined with my mother's, and hers with her mother's, back through the generations, so too are my daughters' lives intertwined with mine. I want Shikha and Maya to know about India, and to feel a sense of belonging to a great tradition. So I read them Indian storybooks and take them to bharat natyam (south Indian classical dance) lessons. I am particularly proud when I see them perform this difficult dance form with skill and grace. They, in turn, give me glimpses into their preoccupations and I learn more about the challenges of growing up in middle-class, White communities. They know they are different from their friends, and when they were younger would feel embarrassed about the Indian food being served at home when their friends visited. Shikha told me our house looked strange—an indirect reference to the Indian artefacts, paintings and ethnic furnishings. Both give me unsolicited tips on how to behave and what to wear. For instance, Shikha would tell me not to call out and wave to someone across the street and Maya insists that I would be better off wearing pants rather than salwar kameez. Shikha was aghast at my wearing bindis and having my nose pierced (this was before Madonna had popularized bindis and 'body-piercing' became the rage in the mid-nineties). While India has been very much a part of our life, there was really little Jewish presence till my mother came to live with us in 1989. Mum made a point of doing seder in our home, and celebrating Hanukkah, and other Jewish festivals.

I agreed to my mother's suggestion that Shikha and Maya attend Jewish Sunday school to learn more about Jewish traditions. Perhaps I have come to understand the significance of my own Jewish heritage because I want to pass it on to my daughters. Sometimes we must travel great distances to come home. I had to leave Calcutta to meet my Calcutta-born, Indian husband. To understand and affirm my Jewish heritage I have had to travel even further through time. I have made this journey through developing this set of portraits—in the process I have come to know another part of me. I now mount these family portraits on a much broader canvas, shifting my narrative into a dialogue with contemporary discourses on colonialism, postcolonialism, nationalism, diaspora, and identity formation for travelling communities.

Notes

Flyleaf: Jael and Amitava at their wedding in Austin, Texas, 1981.
Amitava puts sindoor in the parting of Jael's hair, marking their marriage in traditional Hindu fashion.

1 Nahoum's in the New Market is almost a legend in the Jewish community. Calcutta Jews regularly meet and socialize in the shop and Jews from other parts of the world hear about it and congregate there too. It has been a community space for a long period of time.

2 Jack Jacob, in *Surrender at Dacca: Birth of A Nation* (Delhi: Manohar, 1997), describes his involvement in the campaign for the 'liberation' of

Bangladesh.

3 Though he has made a deep impression on me, I lost touch with him after he left Wellesley College. Many years later I found out that he was awarded the Alternative Nobel Peace Prize. In the early 1990s, on a visit to Chile, I saw his name on billboards in Santiago as one of the Presidential candidates promoting an alternative and green agenda.

4 bell hooks cited by Doreen Massey, 'Double Articulation: A Place in the World' in Bammer (ed.), *Displacements: Cultural Identities in Question*, p. 119.

5 See bell hooks, *Talking Back: Thinking Feminist, Thinking Black* (Boston: Southend Press, 1989).

6 Papusa Molina, 'Recognizing, Accepting and Celebrating our Differences,' in Anzaldua (ed.), *Making Face, Making Soul*, p. 329.

$\mathcal{G}$ RANNY,' I ASKED, 'WHAT ARE YOU?' I was a teenager visiting my grand-mother Mary in London. When I pressed her to tell me her nationality, she answered matter-of-factly: 'Darling, I'm Jewish.' While I argued that 'Jewish' was her religion and not her nationality, she insisted that she was Jewish and nothing else. My grandmother would not be browbeaten into defining herself in terms of a place or a nation—as British, Indian, or Israeli. My grandmother Mary and my great-grandmother Farha lived their lives within the enclaves of a tight-knit Jewish community. They identified solely with the Baghdadi Jewish diaspora community, regardless of its loca-tion on the map. Although my mother stepped outside this world to iden-tify with other communities (national and transnational), I am the first of the four generations of Calcutta Jewish women to think of myself as unam-bivalently Indian. Growing up in an independent and secular India in a pre-dominantly Indian environment, I took my Indian identity as a given.

Most people familiar with India—and most Indians—are at first sur-prised when I say I am Indian. I am fair-skinned, have dark brown wavy hair, and look more Middle-Eastern than Indian. So I explain that I may not look 'typically Indian' (knowing that there is no such thing) because I am Baghdadi Jewish from Calcutta. My explanation usually generates more surprise, and people will tell me that they have never heard of an Indian Jew, much less met one. As soon as I start conversing with another Indian, however, my not-at-first-seeming Indian becomes a non-issue. I think my Indianness was never questioned in Calcutta because Jews, Parsis, Armenians, and Anglo-Indians were part of Calcutta life when I was grow-ing up. Some members of these communities thought of 'home' as some-where else (Anglo-Indians might talk of 'going home' to England;

Armenians, to Armenia); however, I will always think of Calcutta as home, even though I have not lived there since I was sixteen.[1]

I had reached my mid-thirties so sure of my Indianness that it came as a rude shock when a progressive Indian friend challenged my identity. We were at an indigenous women's meeting on a reservation in Montana, listening to Native Americans as they outlined their priorities for political and social action. During one session I doodled an intricate Indian design, and a colleague complimented me on its beauty. When she said, 'Indians are so artistic,' my friend interjected: 'But Jael is not really Indian.' Her callous remark pained me, and I responded sharply: 'Since when have you joined the Jan Sangh?' We both knew what I meant. The Jan Sangh is the Hindu chauvinist party that advocates a Hindu India. It gives voice to Hindu nationalist sentiments and is known for its anti-minority political rhetoric. Although my friend immediately backed off and shamefacedly mumbled an apology of sorts, her remark stayed with me as a symbol of a larger phenomenon, the attempts underway to remake India into a Hindu nation. From the inclusive rhetoric of the anti-colonial leaders after Indian independence and through the 1950s and 1960s, India has experienced a decisive shift to the Hindutva politics that have found expression in the Bharatiya Janata Party (BJP). Not only in the charged communal environment within India, but also among many Indians living in the United States, a narrow view of who is Indian keeps gaining ground.

For the four generations of women from the travelling community portrayed within these pages, personal and community identity has been shaped within shifting environments and amid sweeping historical and cultural changes. For each of us, 'identity' has been more a matter of self-representation than a function of where we were born or the length of time we lived in a particular place. Although Farha and Mary lived in Calcutta for most of their lives, they chose to live as outsiders. My mother, who left India in her forties, identifies herself culturally not only with India but also with Israel and the United States. When I left Calcutta at sixteen, I was the same age as Farha when she arrived. She lived there till she died in her eighties, whereas I return to India only intermittently and will probably never live there again. Still, although I have spent the least time there, I identify more strongly with India than with any other country.

The idea of 'citizenship'— by which I mean, above all, identifying with a place—meant little to my grandmother and great-grandmother. Largely a product of nationalism (a twentieth-century phenomenon in much of the world), the notion of citizenship, an allegiance to a geographic place, had little significance—practical or conceptual—in their lives. Throughout her extensive travels, Farha never needed a passport. A letter of credit from the Hong Kong and Shanghai Bank to the ports she and Saleh visited sufficed. For Mary, citizenship and residency were merely the arbitrary and bureaucratic hurdles she needed to surmount in her relentless attempt to remain part of her travelling community. To emigrate to Australia and later to England and Israel, Mary did need a passport. Because her husband, Elias, was born in Singapore, a Crown Colony, she was a citizen of the United Kingdom and was able to obtain a passport using that designation. With that passport in hand, she was able to continue to be part of the Baghdadi Jewish community as it shifted from Calcutta to new locations.

Farha and Mary embody a notion of 'belonging' that does not correspond to prevailing narratives of nation. A sense of belonging need not come from identifying with the dominant culture; it may also arise from having one's place validated by the larger plural culture of which one is a part and from feeling secure and content with one's place within it. Although Farha and Mary were British subjects by virtue of living in India, they saw themselves as neither British nor Indian. They were Iraqi Jewish women: their identification was with Judaism, a shifting community, and with the memories and practice of their inherited religion and cultural traditions. Thus, in each country in which they lived or visited, they anchored themselves in the life of the Bagdhadi Jewish community. The community was their 'home' and provided them with the material and emotional securities that gave them their sense of belonging. Rooted in the life and rhythms of this community, their Jewishness, their gender, and their class circumscribed their world.

Farha and Mary's travel cannot be separated from the expansion and relocation narrative of the Baghdadi community. Iraqi Jews were not a land-based community. They were a community of mobile traders and business people who, as the times changed, picked up new professions. As members of this mobile community, Farha and Mary dwelled in travelling. The travel of women helped to bind the diaspora communities together through marriage and other social interactions. Women had particular community functions to perform and were key actors in welding these far-flung communities into a unit through forging and maintaining kinship ties.

Travel for women was essentially a community and a family affair rather than an individual's experience with 'otherness'. As a young bride going out to be married in Calcutta in the early twentieth century, Farha was expected to negotiate her way within familiar Baghdadi worlds, not strange countries and environments. Thus, in many ways gender arrangements and norms protected women from directly confronting an alien world in the places where they travelled and lived.

Farha and Mary were at home across vast geographic areas because their movements and travel were part of structured travel circuits linking people at home and away. Their routes were charted by Baghdadi Jews whose wealth, status, community organizations, and networks cushioned their moves. The presence of community made them feel that even though they had travelled to a distant place, their 'home'—the community— remained the same. In each place in different parts of the world, there were people they knew who shared religious customs, foods, and world-views. In contrast, when the men of the Baghdadi Jewish community first came out to India and the Far East, they had to fend for themselves and their families or depend on Jewish charities. Saleh had to negotiate his way through markets and docksides across the Far East. Elias, working at the Calcutta docks, had to negotiate his place among other minority communities as well and soon learned the language skills to do so. Elias also socialized with non-Jews and interacted with a broad cross-section of the Calcutta community.

It was Saleh and Elias, not Farha and Mary, who were thrust into 'contact zones', those spaces that Mary Louise Pratt has defined as 'the space of colonial encounters, the spaces in which people geographically and historically separated come into contact with each other and establish on-going relations, usually involving conditions of coercion, radical inequality and intractable conflict.'[2] Because Saleh and Elias were from a minority trading community and not from the dominant societies of either the colonizer or the colonized, they probably did not experience the inequalities embedded in the notion of the 'contact zone' as starkly as Pratt has presumed. This suggests that ethnicity shaped a complex range of encounters within the contact zones, and gender mediated and shaped the nature of those encounters.

Mary's travel experiences offer a poignant contrast to Farha's. Farha moved up and down the Baghdadi Jewish diaspora—from Basra to

Djakarta—in her early married life as the young wife of a trader. In each of the places she visited, she lived in a familiar world, with limited dealings outside her community. While Saleh and Farha made Calcutta their base, they depended on the diaspora community to provide a safe harbour in the alien surroundings in which they lived and travelled. Mary was wholly immersed in the life of the Baghdadi Jewish community in Calcutta until her middle years, when the community began to dwindle. Although she did all she could as a supervisor in the Jewish Girls' hostel to keep community traditions alive, she felt a sense of loss and displacement as she witnessed the rapid shift of the community to other sites. After her husband's death in Australia, Mary embarked on a prolonged search for home—for a place in the community to which she belonged—because she could only feel some fulfillment when she was at the centre of Jewish community life. This was a time, however, when the centre of community life was itself in motion.

Because the community was relocating, Mary's search was a difficult and wrenching process. When she could not be part of the Baghdadi Jewish community, she suffered a sense of profound alienation. Iraq was now merely the place from which her family came; it was her past but played no role in her present or future. India, Australia, England, and Israel were, successively, her present, while her future was located in spiritual and mystical pursuits that were tied to Jewish lore. Although her Jewish identity was central to her being, the long-established travel circuits that Saleh and Farha had travelled no longer offered the home she sought, for these communities had been reconfigured after the Second World War.

Although Farha and Mary, as members of a diaspora community, travelled across many borders, they both drew firm boundaries in all aspects of their lives. Borders determined their social world, the food they ate and where they ate. They established the distance between them and the non-Jewish worlds that surrounded them. In the heart of the British Empire, Farha and Mary spent their days in Calcutta within an Iraqi Jewish world. For all the years that Farha lived in British India, she spoke only a smattering of English. Comfortable in her wrappers, she never adopted Western-style clothing, and, like other middle-class and poorer Jews, she never mixed with those outside the Jewish community. Although Mary spoke English fluently, wore Western-style clothing, and enjoyed Western popular culture and music, she nevertheless remained an outsider, watching the West from a distance.

Mary organized her life around and lived within the borders she established for herself. My most vivid recollection of my grandmother's border-setting exercises comes from when she lived in my mother's small non-kosher flat in Jerusalem. She had set up the kitchen with her kosher space on one side. She called this the 'East Bank', and humorously warned us not to cross between the 'East' and 'West'. She also organized her life in very rigid and inflexible patterns. No matter where she was, she rose early, did her work scrupulously, spent a lot of time in prayer, crocheted or knitted while chatting or listening to music, wrote letters regularly, and had specific days and times set aside for outings. My mother remembers that when she was growing up she could tell the day of the week from the food that was served. Granny seemed to root herself in the well-regulated routines of her life as well as in the web of family and community relations. This provided her with a sense of continuity and security in the vastly different rooms, located in different places, in which she lived her life.

Border setting and boundary maintenance exercises were not just an individual endeavour, they were also a community endeavour. For it was through community boundary maintenance that community identity was created and upheld. Education, formal and informal community organizations, and networks played an important role in establishing and maintaining community identity and defining the special roles of women. Farha and Mary, in fact, enjoyed considerably greater freedoms in India than they would have in Iraq, which had been more conservative in its cultural orientation. Because life in the diaspora community was less rigid and structured than it had been for her family in Iraq, Mary did not face resistance as she responded to the new educational and career opportunities available in Calcutta. As a middle-class woman living in India, she was able to afford household help. This meant that she could pursue her career and enjoy her leisure time by going to the movies or devoting herself to community and religious activities.

Farha's and Mary's narratives indicate that living in India as a minority community was not a disadvantaged position. The British protected and favoured the minority communities for political reasons. Jews did not face any discrimination in India and were socially well respected. Although Farha and Mary, like most Jewish women, chose to be on the margins of political and social life in India, they were very much at the centre of the affairs of the community. Those Jewish women who sought to be active in politics and social life were, in fact, warmly received and achieved positions of prominence. Jewish women did not face the strictures imposed on most Indian women, nor did they have to fulfil norms expected of British women living in India at the time. The outlines of what was considered proper or improper behaviour for British women were firmly drawn to meet the dictates of Empire. Because middle-class people in the Jewish community did not have to meet Indian or British imperial agendas, they had more space to carve out a place for themselves within the family and in society.

The Jews of India may have identified with British ways, but they did not see themselves as—nor did the British accept them as—Britishers. However, they did not see themselves as 'the colonized' either and did not experience the kind of hatred or low self-esteem that is, according to the analysis of scholars such as Fanon and Memmi, part of the colonized psyche.[3] The lives of Farha and Mary in colonial Calcutta—and that of my mother before Indian independence—suggest that distinct communities of women living in India at different periods experienced and were affected by colonialism in very particular ways.

For all the distances that Farha and Mary travelled overseas, in some ways my mother travelled a far greater distance when she boarded the train for Delhi. She moved from a Baghdadi Jewish to an Indian space, and during her time in Delhi as a student she became part of another, pan-Indian community. The India with which she identified was a secular space, as articulated by the Congress party, where all religions and communities could thrive. The distance she had travelled can be measured by her reception when she returned to Calcutta for a visit in Indian dress, which she had adopted by her second year at Lady Irwin. When Flower stepped off the train at Howrah Station, her mother was horrified to see her beloved Jewish daughter wearing a dusty white salwar kameez: 'My mother was speechless on the long ride home, anger welling up deep within her. I remember stepping out of my bath to find her picking up my Indian clothes, putting them in the dhobi hamper. She said to me in no uncertain terms that as long as I was in her house I was never to wear these clothes. In her subconscious she realized I was wearing these clothes in Delhi. I guess so long as she did not have to see me wear them she could turn a blind eye to this breach of conduct.'

Flower's mother did not disapprove of her nationalist sentiments, but she was very wary about the wearing of Indian clothes. Flower thinks this

Above The Maghen David synagogue seen from the street, 2000. *Below* The interior of the synagogue, 2000.

Above Sefer torah scrolls. *Below* Tandoor oven for baking matzahs in the Beth-el synagogue compound, 2000.

must have sprung from a concern that such outward manifestations of Indianness could lead to marriage outside the community and the loss of Jewish identity. This response to wearing Indian clothes was met by other Jewish girls who wore saris in those times. By the 1940s there were a handful of women in the Jewish community who had married Indians and adopted an Indian lifestyle. They dressed in saris because this was essential for acceptance into their husband's homes and families. Most of the community was disturbed by intermarriage and feared that their children might marry outside the community if they were not strict enough with them.

Wearing Indian clothes was a source of shame for Jewish families, who had by now all adopted Western dress. Several of the minority communities in Calcutta—the Armenians, Parsis, and Anglo Indians—wore Western dress. An aunt on my father's side married into a landed and very conservative Bengali family. She says her father mourned her marriage as though she had died. Many years later, she came to synagogue on Yom Kippur in a sari, which is all she would have been permitted to wear in her in-laws' extended-family household. Her father told her that not only had she shamed him, but she had disgraced him publicly.

Some of the first troubling questions of identity for the Calcutta Jews arose with the onset of World War II. Sally Solomon describes how she felt compelled, for the first time, to define who she was:

> So far, as an individual, I had felt secure, protected, no questions asked, only answerable to my own immediate family, and the larger family of Jews to which I belonged; but now, chinks were beginning to appear in the protective walls, allowing me to look outside those barriers. To begin with, it was not a very comfortable feeling. Answers were needed to questions which I had previously not felt urgent enough to worry about. Are we English? Are we Indian? I did not feel either of these; just thought of myself as Jewish—not so much in a religious sense as belonging to a group identified by its religion. I dressed like the English, spoke their language, embraced some of their ways of life; but neither they nor I would consider I belonged. The same applied to being Indian, but in different areas. I did not adopt their dress, speak their language even reasonably well, yet I belonged more, felt like India was my native place.[4]

Indian independence forced the Calcutta Jewish community to come to terms with their ambivalent sense of identity. The Baghdadi Jews had invested in India, and those who could afford it owned land and commercial enterprises. They knew the language and customs, and had extensive Indian contacts that they were able to use in business. Thus, they were of India, but they did not see themselves as Indian. The in-between-ness of their location in race-based British imperial structures complicates colonial discourses that are conceived of in terms of two analytical categories only—the colonizer or the colonized. Yet, the role of minority communities like the Jews, precisely because of their ambiguity, was essential for the functioning of colonialism and the dictates of Empire. The Jews were intermediaries for the British and through their networks enhanced Calcutta's commercial reach. They were favoured by the British and commercially successful, which made them loyal British subjects. In many ways the situation of the Baghdadi Jews in India was not that different from that of Jewish populations in other colonial locations. Albert Memmi speaks of the situation of Jews in Tunisia, 'eternally hesitant candidates refusing assimilation', in a similar fashion:

> Their constant and very justifiable ambition is to escape from their colonized condition . . . To that end, they endeavor to resemble the colonizer in the frank hope that they may cease to consider them different from him. But if the colonizer does not always openly discourage these candidates to develop that resemblance, he does not permit them to attain it either. Thus, they live in painful and constant ambiguity. Rejected by the colonizer, they share in part of the physical conditions of the colonized and have a communion of interests with them; on the other hand, they reject the values of the colonized as belonging to a decayed world from which they eventually hope to escape.[5]

Homi Bhabha has developed a similar formulation—'almost the same but not quite . . . almost the same but not white'—in his discussion of 'colonial mimicry'.[6] The favoured economic and race status of Calcutta Jews in the British Empire, together with their familiarity with local culture and politics, placed them in a strong position to exercise political choices in the postcolonial period. They were able to realign and relocate themselves in India and overseas with the ending of British rule.

My mother's generation had to resolve their sense of identity individually and as a community. The British never did resolve the Jews' ambiguous status—not quite European, not quite Indian—although, under British rule the Jews identified themselves as Europeans and were loyal British subjects. The Baghdadi Jews had put down roots in India and filled an in-between, ambiguous position, which for the most part, suited their purpose. Their 'home' was India. The Jews only talked metaphorically—in religious terms—of the Holy Land being their spiritual homeland. While it is true that Jews over the centuries have said 'next year in Jerusalem' as part of the seder prayers, they never meant it literally. As a homeland to which Jews could return, Israel only became a reality in the mid-twenti-eth century

Alongside the growth of nationalism in India, since the 1930s a bur-geoning Zionist consciousness was being forged, especially among the Jewish youth. My mother was involved not only in Indian nationalism but in the Zionist movement as well. Habonim was the first and only Zionist youth movement of Calcutta.[7] This group started in the late 1930s under the leadership of Mrs Krieger, a teacher in the Jewish Girls' School. Flower and other students came to know about Zionism from Mrs Krieger, who was sent from Palestine (1939) to teach modern Hebrew. She and her hus-band were active in Habonim in their short two-year stay in Calcutta. They had to return to Palestine before the Japanese invasion of Burma, and after they left, others picked up their work. Hebrew was promoted as a spoken language, and Habonim worked to inculcate dedication to the Zionist cause. Most of Habonim's work revolved around education—teach-ing folk songs and dances, and the ways of life in Palestine.

The work of Habonim greatly expanded Calcutta Jewish horizons. Habonim collected funds for the blue boxes (money to support Israel) from the broader community. The younger members of the community were idealistic, and some committed themselves to the Zionist cause. The eld-ers of the community for the most part just watched these political devel-opments unfold. Just as they were uninvolved in Indian politics, so they remained uncommitted and uninvolved in Zionist politics. These Jews had never before considered an actual return to the 'homeland', and thus, even when many had a choice to leave India and go to Israel, most of the com-munity—except for a few young idealists inspired by Habonim—did not exercise this choice. Baghdadi Jews of India did not feel the need for a Jewish state in order to pursue their religious way of life, nor was it nec-essary to them for their survival as a people.

While my great-grandmother and grandmother's worlds were shaped by the Baghdadi Jewish diaspora and British colonialism, my mother's world was shaped by the demise of British colonialism, and the emergence of Jewish and Indian nationalism. When she returned to Calcutta in 1949 after completing her undergraduate degree, she found significant changes underway. In these short but tumultuous three years, many of her relatives had left for London, Israel, and Australia, while others were getting ready to leave. The first group of Jews to leave Calcutta in the late 1940s were about 20 'GI brides'. They were part of a larger group of predominantly Anglo-Indian and British brides from Calcutta. This large group of women sailed to join their American soldier husbands, who had been stationed in Calcutta and the surrounding areas during the War. Shortly after, Jewish refugees from Burma began to emigrate to the United States because they had priority in the quota system. An idealistic group of young men and women from Habonim emigrated to Palestine to join the kibbutz movement. The small Jewish community thus began unravelling. From their insular and cohesive world in Calcutta they voluntarily emigrated to all parts of the globe.

Even though many of them had developed a sense of belonging to India, most Calcutta Jews feared what the future might hold without the British in command, because that was the only India they knew. They were sceptical of what life would be like in an 'Indian India'. Having lived always in a British India, they did not know how much they would have to change their ways if India attained independence. When I asked older members of the community what they had feared would happen when the British left, they recalled their often unstated apprehensions. Some worried about the possibility of having to conduct all their business in Hindi, which would have been difficult for them, for English had become their first language. They were comfortable in spoken Hindustani but not fluent in spoken or written Hindi. Others thought they might have to become more Indian in their ways. They wondered whether they would have to wear only Indian clothes. The more wealthy Jews were unsure of monetary restrictions that the new government might impose, making it difficult to take their money out of India should they need to do so. Although in retrospect many of these fears may appear unfounded or trivial, they were nevertheless among the reasons that many Jews left Calcutta. While they had these very practical concerns, there was never any fear of anti-Semitism from Muslims and Hindus in India. The new constitution of India, which was being debated and framed at the time, further reassured them. It envisioned India as a secular state that respected the freedom of all communities to practice their religions. While tensions between Hindus and Muslims ran high, the Jews did not feel threatened by either community.

A few among my mother's generation, including my mother, who were very Western in their orientation and comfortable in that world (as opposed to Mary's generation which had stood between a Judeo-Arab and a Judeo-British identity), saw their 'communion of interests' with India as it sought its place in the parade of nations. They identified with the 'modern' and 'secular' elements of the national movement. Thus, most the Jews who stayed on supported the Congress party, confident that it could lead India forward into a new era of progress and prosperity. Others in the Jewish community from this generation saw their communion of interest with other Jews who were working towards the creation of Israel. The majority, however, saw their economic and professional future in the British Commonwealth and so emigrated to England, Canada, and Australia. Some went to the United States if they were accepted through the quota system.

Members of the Jewish community who opted to stay on—like my mother—experienced the idealism and exhilaration, along with the turmoil and pain, of the transition from colonial to postcolonial citizenship, living in a differently constructed world. In the first decade after independence India was in the process of reconstituting itself as an independent nation. Flower recounts: 'Returning to Calcutta after the exhilarating days of nationalism in Delhi, I was very proud to be part of the present, and determined to follow Gandhi's dreams of a New India.' She and the country alike were engaged in the process of deforming/reforming their identity. Arjun Appadurai succinctly captures the constant negotiations that have to be made in the decolonization process: 'For the former colony, decolonization is a dialogue with the colonial past, and not a simple dismantling of colonial habits and modes of life . . . In the Indian case, the cultural aspects of decolonization affect every domain of public life . . . In every major public debate in contemporary India, one underlying strand is always the question of what to do with the shreds and patches of the colonial heritage. Some of these patches are institutional; others are ideological and aesthetic.'[8]

The new Indian government, committed to a strong anti-imperialist stance, extended Gandhi's campaign of swadeshi (using Indian goods and boycotting foreign ones) to safeguard India from foreign domination. Espousing an Indian brand of socialism, Nehru was committed to developing India's industrial capacity and hailed the Soviet Union as the model to be emulated in India's drive for self-sufficiency.[9] Citizens, in the spirit of sacrifice and patriotism, were to eschew imported goods. As a consequence of these policies, British and foreign goods that had been freely available disappeared from the market over a five-year period. My mother recalls the changes: 'Gradually, fewer imported goods reached us. It took time for Indian-made products to come up to par with imported goods. Matches did not light, and khadi replaced fine crepe-de-chine. Olives, chocolates, cheese and asparagus, that we bought freely, suddenly were available only on the black market and we paid the higher prices for them when we needed them.' In fact, this transition process fuelled a craving for imported goods and bred an attitude that Indian goods were inferior. This attitude towards 'Made in India', a colonial hangover, was difficult to eradicate even as India's industrial and manufacturing capacity grew.[10]

Throughout the 1950s and 1960s Indianization was taking place in all facets of Calcutta life. Schools, for instance, became more Indianized in their outlook and curriculum. Hindi became a compulsory language even in the Jewish Girls' School, where non-Jewish students were now accepted. By the mid-1960s most of the teachers were non-Jewish because most Jews had left Calcutta, and the headmistress was a Bengali woman who wore a sari to school. Clubs that had been exclusively European were opened to Indian members. My mother recalls a clumsy attempt to negotiate an Indian identity, when my father, in a spirit of defiance, wore a formal Indian jacket and churidars (tight-fitted leggings) to a black-tie function at a swanky restaurant. The restaurant, which had formerly catered to Europeans and now catered to Indians, still maintained British dress codes and other formalities, and refused entry to my father.

My mother also remembers how 'dishes like tandoori chicken appeared on the menus of most clubs and restaurants in place of boneless chicken and smoked hilsa (a fish delicacy). Clubs started serving *pakoras* and *samosas* and *naan* in lieu of chicken or cucumber sandwiches.' Uma Narayan analyses the ways in which food is 'linked to issues of identity, prestige, social place and symbolic meaning.' She contends that food plays a role in 'the scripts of Nation and national identity' and argues that food reveals a great deal about 'how we understand our personal and collective identities.'[11]

Food symbolizes the ways in which aspects of the colonial period were accepted, rejected or incorporated in the identity building process.

Attempts to determine and assert an identity and to negotiate the colonial past are most intense in the period directly after colonialism ends, as this is the time when anxieties regarding who you are and what you want to be are heightened. In the process of self-determination there are contradictions and difficulties in attaining meaningful transformations from a colonial to an independent identity. Appadurai, in an essay on the Indianization of cricket, introduces the notion of 'hard' versus 'soft' cultural images and notes the difficulty of transforming the former. Furthermore he makes a useful distinction between them: 'Hard cultural forms are those that come with a set of links between value, meaning and embodied practice that are difficult to break and hard to transform. Soft cultural forms, by contrast are those that permit relatively easy separation of embodied performance from meaning and value, and relatively successful transformation at each level.'[12] I find this concept useful in articulating and exploring the challenges my mother's generation confronted in their attempts to shift their identity from a colonial to an Indian one.

My parent's generation awkwardly navigated these 'hard' and 'soft' cultural changes intrinsic to the process of decolonization. Let us take the example of that colonial, British-influenced institution, the club. The clubs, in a self-conscious attempt to Indianize, have bearers serve hot *pakoras* rather than cucumber sandwiches at teatime. While this certainly does mark a cultural shift, it is a very limited shift. The change to *pakoras*, a soft cultural form, uneasily overlays a hard colonial form—the British custom of tea time at the club. The club was not transformed from a colonial space to an Indian one even though the members and the food served were now Indian. Rather, tea time at the club is a hard cultural form that 'changes those who are socialized into it more readily than it is itself changed.'[13] Wearing an achkan or serving *pakoras* could not break the links between value, meaning and embodied practice. These contradictory and complicated negotiations in which the colonized engage are filled with cultural meaning. It is in this cultural crucible that colonial vestiges and undertones continue, in a mutated form, in many parts of Calcutta life.

Western holidays like Christmas, New Year, and Easter receded into the background, but never quite went away. Mummy recalls a Christmas when she was about five years old: 'My parents took me to see the

Christmas pageant at Whiteway Laidlaw and Co., which was a large British-owned department store. Christmas trees, Santa and a sledge, plum pud-dings and mince pies created a little bit of London in Calcutta. Anglo-Indians and Britishers came from all over the region, from as far away as Dacca, to shop and admire its splendour.' When I was about her age I remember Dad taking us for a drive down Park Street, a fashionable com-mercial street in south Calcutta, to see it all lit up for Christmas. We admired the festive lights, the decorated trees and the stars in many shop windows. By the time I was an adult Christmas was hardly noticeable even on Park Street, except for the few telltale signs outside restaurants announcing a Christmas dance or lunch. On the other hand, I recall cele-brating Diwali and Holi, both north Indian Hindu festivals, with great verve.

Although among the Jews who had stayed behind there were those, like my parents and many of their Westernized Indian friends, who felt patriotic about and invested in the new India, they nevertheless remained anchored to their colonial moorings. They lived in the Westernized part of the city and were most at ease in the more Anglicized southern part of Calcutta—what was once the White town. The Anglicized social spaces like the clubs, the (horse) race course, and the New Market are still the areas where they gather. In addition to the wealthier Jews some of the very old members of the community also stayed on. The wealthier and the eld-erly Jews were comfortable where they were and not willing to make the necessary adjustment to living overseas. The poor stayed on for a while, but over the years they were sponsored by Israel and emigrated because Israel offered them better economic opportunities. By the early 1960s, when I was growing up, there were only a few hundred Jews left in Calcutta. As a result, the Calcutta I grew up in was fundamentally differ-ent, with a different cultural axis, than it had been for my foremothers. Whereas Farha and Mary's experience of Calcutta was a colonial one, the experiences my mother and I had in Calcutta were predominantly post-colonial. I was immersed in and surrounded by an independent India and much less exposed to the West than they had been, though faded vestiges of Calcutta's colonial past still remained. Furthermore, my generation did not feel the anxiety my parent's generation felt as they shifted from colo-nial rule to become citizens of an independent nation. My generation could take being Indian for granted.

Whereas Farha and Mary were very much part of transnational

Baghdadi Jewish circuits and colonial networks, Flower grew up in the Baghdadi Jewish world of Calcutta and is still connected to some members of the Baghdadi community. Yet she has lived all of her adult life outside the Baghdadi Jewish diaspora, which she is adept at navigating. For me the Baghdadi Jewish community is a faint memory that came alive for me only through this writing. My mother and I travelled as individuals, beyond community circuits.

It is important to include the temporal as well as the spatial movements undertaken by individuals. I believe my mother and I travelled the furthest—moved the greatest distance from where we were psychologically located when we moved within India. I underline the point that though Flower travelled to many countries in the latter part of her life she never travelled as far as she did when she moved from Calcutta to Delhi. In each of the places she lived thereafter, England, Israel and the United States, the worlds where she lived were shaped by the global mass culture spawned by the colonial encounter. Stuart Hall notes the distinguishing features of this mass culture. It is centred in the West and speaks English as an international language that is distinct from the Queen's English but still centred in the languages of the West. It also practises a peculiar form of homogenization that never aims for totality but recognizes and absorbs 'differences within the larger, over-arching framework of what is essentially an American conception of the world.'[14] Since childhood Flower was immersed in this global cultural flow and in each place she lived she tapped into it and imbibed local influences. For example, her class background and her Anglo moorings enabled her to engage with the global flow of images, news, and opinions that she shared with other privileged members of her translocal community in Jerusalem. She was never part of mainstream Israeli culture and society, but the familiar Anglo cultural current in which she immersed herself in Jerusalem provided a sense of belonging. In this translocality she did not feel overwhelmed or marginalized by the dominant Israeli culture. Thus in three very distinct countries she lived within communities that have long been interconnected and propelled by the same powerful sets of global forces. This sameness across countries and cultures makes us rethink our polarized and nation-based notions of the world, emphasizing the cultural power and hegemony of colonialism and post-colonial forces.[15] These forces, emanating from the West, have exerted so much power that they have shaped other countries and cultures and brought significant segments of those cultures under their sway. They explain the fact that the community in which Flower lived in colonial and postcolonial Calcutta is not culturally that different from the community of which she is now a part in Iowa City.

My most significant travel experience was when I crossed class lines within India. In Udaipur, where I lived with few class or economic privileges, I had a glimpse of what it is like to live as a lower-class or poor person in an Indian context. It forever changed the way I understood the world around me. My mother's travel experiences within India, and my own, demonstrate that the essence of travel is the extent to which one can put oneself into the other's world. Like my foremothers I have found that I travel in small worlds. While they travelled within Baghdadi Jewish worlds and spaces carved out through colonial cultural penetration, I have travelled among a group of people in different parts of the world who are often from similar class and educational backgrounds, share this common culture and worldview, and often have more in common with one another than poor people in the countries where they live. Concepts of travel thus need to be expanded to incorporate the psychological and cultural distances individuals cover rather than just the geographical ones.

While Farha and Mary's transnational identity was Baghdadi Jewish, and my mother's was based on her Jewishness and her familiarity with Western culture, my transnational identity is political. I embraced a third world feminist identity that has remained central to me since my years as a college student in the United States. While I am the first to have openly claimed my feminism, all three of my foremothers were strong-willed, independent women who forged their own paths. Each fended for herself when circumstances were such that she could not rely on the continued support of her husband. Farha became a businesswoman and supported her children when Saleh died, leaving her several children to look after. Mary trained to be a teacher in the early twentieth century when few women of her background and class sought to have a profession. She worked throughout her life and supported herself when Elias's small pension ran out. Mummy worked as a teacher in Calcutta and thus ensured herself some measure of financial independence. She challenged dominant norms for women when she left my father and made a new life for herself in Israel with only very meagre financial backing from him. All three women negotiated their own ways in worlds that were unfamiliar to them. This book is a history of and tribute to these and other such women whose lives and contributions have not been included in historical accounts.

At the start of the twenty-first century, definitions of who is and who is not an Indian are being increasingly politicized, the identities of place are being essentialized and secular forces are increasingly challenged. In this political context minority narratives such as this one have an especially important place. They resist efforts that seek to communalize India's past and present and contrast sharply with contemporary histories in India today that are being rewritten to serve communal politics. This minority diaspora narrative testifies to India's plural past, where many communities flourished. It not only confounds and enriches this past but is relevant to India's present and future. Though the Calcutta Jews were small in number they played a significant role in shaping the cultural and economic contours of Calcutta. Calcutta's identity was extroverted—it was moulded by many different communities and was a product of interactions with the outside world.

The stories also challenge and extend some of the contemporary discourses about diasporas and travel. These stories flesh out the conditions and mechanisms that enable a 'diaspora of hope' to emerge. This Jewish diaspora experience demonstrates that the European Jewish experience cannot be generalized to other Jewish communities. In order not to frame the European Jewish experience as the central Jewish experience I did not want to contrast the two experiences but to have this community understood on its own terms. Diasporic processes are usually framed in terms of overwhelming loss, exile and displacement. This account shows that diaspora narratives are very varied and can be as much about mobility and gain. Through this diaspora experience in India and the Far East and then through its subsequent location to the West, members of this reconstituted diaspora continue to thrive. The travel circuits that the community members traversed facilitated the economic and social prosperity of its members. These same networks supported community members in subsequent relocations.

I have borrowed Clifford's phrase 'dwelling in travelling' and through the stories have shown how this was enacted.[16] I suggest that the ability to 'dwell in travelling'—that is, to conceive of travel as part of sustaining community over large spaces—was critical for feeling a sense of security in alien surroundings. The strategy of distancing oneself from the alien surrounding by building and maintaining invisible borders between one's community and the outside world was essential to feel a sense of home no matter where, or how temporarily, one was located geographically. Daily routines and a strict adherence to a set of beliefs are critical to giving a mobile community a sense of place.

Writing this gendered ethno-history has been a 'crossing the line ceremony' for me—I look back on the past from a new location and see myself in a new place as a result of this crossing. A voyage by ship from India to England that I undertook as a child of ten captures the significance of this crossing. I learned to steer the ship, and spent hours on the upper deck talking and asking questions of the presiding officer. My siblings and I made arrangements with the indulgent officers and cadets on this cargo ship for a traditional 'crossing the line' ceremony as we neared the equator. This customary practice at sea was an exciting event for us children: I expected to see some sort of line or marker on the high seas at the appropriate time. Anticipating this moment on the upper deck I was immensely disappointed when the captain ceremoniously announced that we had just crossed the equator, for I could not make out any visible difference. Except for the ceremony, I would not have known. Looking back I see this marked yet unmarked crossing as a metaphor for all the lines and borders I have crossed knowingly and unknowingly throughout my life. Tracing the religious, cultural, social, geographic and psychological borders the women in my family and I have crossed, I deliberately mark these unmarked crossings to make meaning of their lives and sense of their worlds.

Notes

Flyleaf: Illuminated ketubah or Jewish marriage contract for the marriage, in Beth-el synagogue, of Hannah Khatoon Solomon from Calcutta with Pinhas Elias Hallen of Cochin. The colonial imagery (lion, unicorn, crown and roses) indicates that the marriage was consecrated under the aegis of the British Raj.

1 Here I refer to home as a set of material and emotional securities, but realize the dissonance between place and desire as underlined in cultural criticism today. Cultural critics remind us of why it is important not to give in to ruling ideas of 'total mobility and universal abandon, but also not dreaming of permanent and secure dwellings in the context of strict border-surveillance and severe passport controls. Belonging cannot be housed within the material space of walls and roofs, of fenced topographies and well-drawn maps'—Anne McClintock, Aamir Mufti and Ella Shohat (eds.), *Dangerous Liaisons: Gender, Nation and Postcolonial Perspectives* (Minneapolis: University of Minnesota Press, 1997), p. 1. Being from Calcutta and living outside in the West, I am constantly

reminded that the city is emblematic of poverty and degradation—it is the proverbial 'Black Hole.' Many Western accounts dwell on its hellish qualities. Ward Morehouse notes: 'The truth is that almost everything popularly associated with Calcutta is highly unpleasant and sometimes very nasty indeed. It is bracketed in the Western mind with distant rumors of appalling disaster, riot and degradation'—quoted in John Hutnyk, *The Rumour of Calcutta: Tourism, Charity and the Poverty of Representation* (London: Zed Press, 1996), p. 91.

Neither the exotic, sanitized colonial version nor the impoverished representations do justice to the City. Jyoti Basu, the longstanding ex-Chief Minister of West Bengal best captures what Calcutta means for an insider and very privileged citizen: 'It is a great city noted for its social interactions, political struggles, cultural activities and progressive movements' (Hutnyk, *The Rumour of Calcutta*, quoting a Department of Tourism brochure, p. 93). To me, Calcutta will always be home.

2 Pratt, *Imperial Eyes*, p. 7.

3 See Frantz Fanon, *Wretched of the Earth* (New York: Grove and Weidenfeld, 1963) or *Black Skin, White Masks* (New York: Grove and Weidenfeld, 1967) and Memmi, *The Colonizer and the Colonized*.

4 Solomon, *Hooghly Tales,* p. 119.

5 Memmi, *The Colonizer and the Colonized,* p. 15–6

6 Homi Bhabha, *The Location of Culture* (London/New York: Routledge, 1994), pp. 85–92.

7 Habonim was a Jewish youth group whose name means 'the builders', a reference to those who build the state of Israel.

8 Appadurai, *Modernity at Large*, p. 89.

9 Nehru admired the Soviet Union for bringing about the industrialization of a feudal and backward state and believed it was a valuable model for India's economic development. Through central planning and state control of industry and the economy, Nehruvian Socialism believed that India would be able to usher in prosperity while ensuring equitable income distribution. For the first two decades of India's independence there was a commitment to secularism, democratic institution building, non-alignment and socialist economics.

10 The Indian pop singer Alisha has a hit song called 'Made in India' in which she extols the virtues of the heart of a person 'made in India'. This is a dominant theme in the popular culture of today and is echoed in cinema and the popular media. However, it has taken almost five decades

for this strident confidence in India to emerge.

11 Uma Narayan, *Dislocating Cultures: Identities, Traditions, and Third World Feminism* (New York: Routledge, 1997), p. 161.

12 Appadurai, *Modernity At Large,* p. 90.

13 Ibid.

14 Stuart Hall, 'The Local and the Global: Globalization and Ethnicity' in McClintock et al (eds.), *Dangerous Liaisons,* p. 179.

15 Arif Dirlik, in 'The Postcolonial Aura: Third World Criticism in the Age of Global Capitalism' discusses how the term postcolonial has a multiplicity of meanings. It is used as a literal description of conditions in former colonial societies, it describes the global condition after the period of colonialism and it is used 'to describe a discourse on the above conditions that is informed by the epistemological orientations that are products of those conditions.' In McClintock et al (eds.), *Dangerous Liaisons,* p. 502. I use the term in all of these ways.

16 Clifford, *Routes.* I have drawn extensively upon Clifford's work on travelling cultures and been fascinated with the questions he raises on the different mobilities of men and women, and what counts as 'travel' for men and women in different settings. Clifford's questions regarding whether pilgrimage, family visits or running a stall in a market town (often women's experiences) were considered 'travel' were provocative. His exploratory discussion of the common experience of women staying home and men going abroad, and the impact of this on how 'home' was conceived 'in relation to practices of coming and going' was insightful (p. 6). Finally, his juxtaposition of women's dwelling with men's travelling enabled me to conceive of how the women I was writing about were in fact able to bring travelling and dwelling together in their lives. For a rich discussion on this subject, see the Prologue of Clifford, *Routes* (pp. 1–13).

References

ABRAHAM, Margaret. 'Marginalization and Disintegration of Community Identity among the Jews of India'. In Nathan Katz (ed.) *Studies of Indian Jewish Identity*. New Delhi: Manohar Publishers and Distributors, 1995.

ABU-LUGHOD, Janet L. *Before European Hegemony: The World System A.D. 1250-1350*. New York: Oxford University Press, 1989.

ABU-LUGHOD, Lila. *Writing Women's Worlds: Bedouin Stories*. Berkeley: University of California Press, 1993.

ALCALAY, Ammiel. *After Jews and Arabs: Remaking Levantine Culture*. Minneapolis: University of Minnesota Press, 1993.

ANDERSON, Benedict. *Imagined Communities*. London: Verso, 1991.

ANZALDUA, Gloria (ed.) *Making Face, Making Soul: Creative and Critical Perspectives by Feminists of Color*. San Francisco: Aunt Lute Books, 1990.

APPADURAI, Arjun. *Modernity at Large: Cultural Dimensions of Globalization*. Minneapolis: University of Minnesota Press, 1996.

APPIAH, Kwame. 'Racisms' in David Theo Goldberg (ed.) *Anatomy of Racism*. Minneapolis: University of Minnesota Press, 1990.

BAMMER, Angelika. 'Mother Tongues and Other Strangers: Writing Family across Cultural Divides'. In Angelika Bammer (ed.) *Displacements: Cultural Identities in Question*. Bloomington/Indianapolis: Indiana University Press, 1994.

BARNOUW and KRISHNASWAMY. *Indian Film*. New York: Columbia University Press, 1963.

BEHAR, Ruth. *Translated Woman*. Boston: Beacon Press, 1993.

BHABHA, Homi K. *The Location of Culture*. New York/London: Routledge, 1994.

BHASIN, Kamla and Ritu Menon. *Borders and Boundaries: Women in India's Partition*. New Delhi: Kali for Women, 1998.

BOSE, Sugato and Ayesha Jalal. *Modern South Asia: History, Culture, Political Economy*. New Delhi: Oxford University Press, 1999.

CERNEA, Ruth Fredman. 'Promised Land and Domestic Arguments: The Conditions of Jewish Identity in Burma'. In Nathan Katz (ed.) *Studies of Indian Jewish Identity*. New Delhi: Manohar Publishers and Distributors, 1995.

CHAKRAVARTY, Sumita S. *National Identity in Indian Popular Cinema, 1947-1987*. Austin: University of Texas Press, 1993.

CHAUDHURI Sukanta (ed.). *Calcutta the Living City: Volume 1: The Past*. Calcutta: Oxford University Press, 1990.

CLIFF, Michelle. 'History as Fiction, Fiction as History'. In Rosellen Brown (ed.) *Ploughshares*, 196-203. Vol. 20 (Fall 1994). Nos. 2 & 3.

CLIFFORD, James. 'Diasporas' in *Cultural Anthropology*, 302-38. Vol. 9 (1994). No. 3.

———. *Routes: Travel and Translation in the Late Twentieth Century*. Cambridge, MA: Harvard University Press, 1997.

COLLINS, Patricia Hill. *Black Feminist Thought: Knowledge, Consciousness and the Politics of Empowerment*. New York/London: Routledge, 1990.

COURTER, Gay. *Flowers in the Blood*, New York: Dutton, 1990.

DAVID, Esther. *Walled City*. Madras: Manas, 1997.

DIRLIK, Arif. 'The Postcolonial Aura: Third World Criticism in the Age of Global Capitalism'. In Anne McClintock, Aamir Mufti and Ella Shohat (eds.) *Dangerous Liaisons: Gender, Nation and Postcolonial Perspectives*. Minneapolis: University of Minnesota Press, 1997.

ELIAS, Flower. *The Jews of Calcutta: The Autobiography of a Community, 1798-1972*. Calcutta: The Jewish Association of Calcutta, 1974.

EVERETT, Jana Matson. *Women and Social Change in India*. New Delhi: Heritage Publishers, 1979.

EZRA, Esmond David. *Turning Back the Pages: A Chronicle of Calcutta Jewry*. Vols. I and II, London: Brookside Press, 1986.

FRANTZ Fanon. *Wretched of the Earth*. New York: Grove and Weidenfeld, 1963.

———. *Black Skin, White Masks*. New York: Grove and Weidenfeld, 1967.

GILROY, Paul. *The Black Atlantic: Modernity and Double Consciousness*. Cambridge, MA: Harvard University Press, 1993.

GREWAL, Inderpal. *Home and Harem: Nation, Gender, Empire and the Cultures of Travel*. Durham, NC: Duke University Press, 1996.

GUPTA, Akhil and James Ferguson. *Culture, Power, Place: Explorations in Critical Anthropology*. Durham, NC: Duke University Press, 1997.

HALL, Stuart. 'The Local and the Global: Globalization and Ethnicity'. In Anne McClintock et al (eds.) *Dangerous Liaisons: Gender, Nation and Postcolonial Perspectives*. Minneapolis: University of Minnesota Press, 1997.

HARSTOCK, Nancy. 'Foucault on Power: A Theory for Women?' In Linda J. Nicholson (ed.) *From Feminism to Postmodernism*. New York: Routledge, 1990.

HASAN, Mushirul. *India's Partition: Process, Strategy and Mobilization*. New Delhi: Oxford University Press, 1993.

HOOKS, bell. *Talking Back: Thinking Feminist, Thinking Black*. Boston: Southend Press, 1989.

HUTNYK, John. *The Rumour of Calcutta: Tourism, Charity and the Poverty of Representation*. London: Zed Books, 1996.

HYMAN, Mavis. *Jews of the Raj*. London: Hyman Publishers, 1995.

JACKSON, Stanley. *The Sassoons*. New York: E. P. Dutton & Co. Inc.,1968.

JACOB, Jack. *Surrender at Dacca: Birth of a Nation*. New Delhi: Manohar Publishers and Distributors, 1997.

KAPLAN, Caren. *Question of Travel: Postmodern Discourses of Displacement*. Durham, NC: Duke University Press, 1996.

KATZ, Nathan (ed.) *Studies of Indian Jewish Identity*. New Delhi: Manohar Publishers and Distributors, 1995.

KIRSHENBLATT-GIMBLETT, Barbara. 'Spaces of Dispersal'. In *Cultural Anthropology*, 339-44. Vol. 9 (1994). No 3.

KUMAR, Radha, *The History of Doing*. London: Verso, 1993.

LUHRMANN, T. M. *The Good Parsi: The Fate of the Colonial Elite in a Postcolonial Society*. Cambridge, MA: Harvard University Press, 1996.

MASSEY, Doreen. *Space, Place and Gender*. Minneapolis: University of Minnesota Press, 1994.

———. 'Double Articulation: A Place in the World' in Angelika Bammer (ed.) *Displacements: Cultural Identities in Question*. Indianapolis: Indiana University Press, 1994.

McCLINTOCK, Anne, Aamir Mufti and Ella Shohat (eds.). *Dangerous Liaisons: Gender, Nation and Postcolonial Perspectives*. Minneapolis: University of Minnesota Press, 1997.

MEMMI, Albert. *The Colonizer and the Colonized*. Boston: Beacon Press, 1967.

MINHA, Trinh, T. 'Not You/Like You: Post-Colonial Women and the Interlocking Question of Identity and Difference'. In G. Anzaldua (ed.) *Making Face, Making Soul: Creative and Critical Perspectives by Feminists of Color*. San Francisco: Aunt Lute Books, 1990.

MISHRA, Vijay. 'The Diasporic Imaginary: Theorizing the Indian Diaspora'. In *Textual Practice*, 421-47. Vol. 10 (1996). No. 3.

MOHANTY, Chandra. 'On Being South Asian in North America'. In Paula S Rothenberg (ed.) *Race, Class and Gender in the United States*. New York: St. Martin's Press, 1998.

MOLINA, Papusa. 'Recognizing, Accepting and Celebrating Our Differences'. In G. Anzaldua (ed.) *Making Face, Making Soul: Creative and Critical Perspectives by Feminists of Color*. San Francisco: Aunt Lute Books, 1990.

MUSLEAH, Ezekiel N. *On the Banks of the Ganga: The Sojourn of the Jews in Calcutta*. North Quincy, MA: Christopher Publishing House, 1975.

NANDY, Ashis. *The Intimate Enemy: Loss and Recovery of Self under Colonialism*. New Delhi: Oxford University Press, 1983.

NARAYAN, Uma. *Dislocating Cultures: Identities, Traditions, and Third World Feminism*. New York: Routledge, 1997.

PARKER, Andrew. In Russo Mary, Sommer Doris, and Yaeger Patricia (eds.) *Nationalism and Sexualities*. New York: Routledge, 1992.

PEISS, Kathy. *Cheap Amusements: Working Women and Leisure in Turn-of-the Century New York*. Philadelphia: Temple University Press, 1986.

PRATT, Mary Louise. *Imperial Eyes: Travel Writing and Transculturation*. London: Routledge, 1992.

RAM, P. R. (ed.) *Secular Challenges to Communal Politics: A Reader*. Mumbai: Vikas Adhyayan Kendra, 1998.

RAY, Nisith Ranjan. *Calcutta: The Profile of a City*. Calcutta: K. P. Bagchi & Co., 1986.

ROLAND, Joan G. *Jews in British India: Identity in a Colonial Era*. Hanover, NH: University Press of New England, 1989.

RUSHDIE, Salman. *Imaginary Homelands*. London: Granta Books, 1991.

——. *The Moor's Last Sigh*. New York/London: Pantheon, 1995.

SCHEINDLIN, Raymond P. *A Short History of the Jewish People From Legendary Times to Modern Statehood.* New York: Macmillan, 1998.

SCHERMERHORN, R. A. *Ethnic Plurality in India.* Arizona: University of Arizona Press, 1978.

SHANKAR, S. *Textual Traffic: Colonialism, Modernity and the Economy of the Text.* Albany, NY: State University of New York Press, 2001.

SILLIMAN, Jael. 'Crossing Borders, Maintaining Boundaries: The Life and Times of Farha, a Woman of the Baghdadi Jewish Diaspora 1870-1958'. In *Journal of Indo-Judaic Studies*, 57-79. Vol. 1 (April 1998). No.1.

———. 'Making the Connections: Environmental Justice and the Women's Health Movement'. In *The Journal of Race, Gender and Class*, 104-29. Vol. 5 (1997). No. 1.

——— and Annanya Bhattacharjee. 'Relocating Women's Studies and Activism': A Dialogue. In *Women's Studies and Activism: Theories and Practice. Women's Studies Quarterly*, 122-36. Vol. 27 (Fall/Winter 1999). No. 3/4.

SINHA, Pradip. *Calcutta in Urban History.* Calcutta: Firma KLM Private Limited, 1978.

———. 'Calcutta and the Currents of History 1690-1912'. In Sukanta Chaudhuri (ed.) *Calcutta the Living City: Volume 1: The Past.* Calcutta: Oxford University Press, 1990.

SLAPAK, Orpa. (ed.) *The Jews of India: A Story of Three Communities.* Jerusalem: The Israel Museum, 1995.

SOLOMON, Sally. *Hooghly Tales.* London: David Ashley Publishing, 1998.

SPIVAK, Gayatri Chakravorty. 'Diasporas Old and New: Women in the Transnational World'. In *Textual Practice*, 245-69. Vol. 10 (1996). No. 2.

STRATTON, Jon. 'The Impossible Ethnic: Jews and Multiculturalism in Australia'. In *Diaspora*, 339-73. Vol. 5 (Winter 1996). No. 3.

———. 'The. Colour of Jews: Jews, Race and the White Australia Policy'. *Journal of Australian Studies*, 51-65. 1996. Nos. 50/51.

——— and Ien Ang. 'On Not Speaking Chinese: Postmodern Ethnicity and the Politics of Diaspora.' In *New Formations*, 1-19. Winter 1994. No. 24.

TAX, Meredith. 'The Power of the Word'. In Jael Silliman and Ynestra King (eds.) *Dangerous Intersections: Feminist Perspectives on Population,*

Environment and Development. Cambridge, MA: South End Press, 1999.

THAROOR, Tilottama (ed.) *Naari*. Calcutta: Ladies Study Group, 1990.

THORNTON, John. *Africa and Africans in the Making of the Atlantic World 1400-1680*. Cambridge: Cambridge University Press, 1996.

TIMBERG, Thomas A. 'Indigenous and Non-Indigenous Jews'. In Nathan Katz (ed.) *Studies of Indian Jewish Identity*. New Delhi: Manohar Publishers and Distributors, 1995.

VISWANATHAN, Gauri. 'Currying Favor: The Politics of British Educational and Cultural Policy in India, 1813-1854'. In Anne McClintock et al (eds.) *Dangerous Liaisons: Gender, Nation and Postcolonial Perspectives*. Minneapolis: University of Minnesota Press, 1997.

WATSON, Julia and Sidonie Smith. *Decolonizing the Subject: The Politics of Gender in Women's Autobiography*. Minneapolis: University of Minnesota Press, 1992.

WOLFF, Janet. *Feminine Sentences: Essays on Women and Culture*. Berkeley: University of California Press, 1990.

WOLPERT, Stanley. *A New History of India*. New York/Oxford: Oxford University Press, 1993.

Index